a Ron

MILLSTONE GRIT

By the same author:

Neighbours (poems) (1970)
Rest The Poor Struggler (poems) (1972)

MILLSTONE GRIT

Glyn Hughes

READERS UNION
Group of Book Clubs
Newton Abbot 1975

First published by Victor Gollancz Ltd

This edition was produced in 1975 for sale to its members
only by the proprietors, Readers Union Limited,
P O Box 6, Newton Abbot, Devon, TQ12 2DW.
Full details of membership will gladly be sent on request

Reproduced and printed in Great Britain
by Redwood Burn Limited
Trowbridge & Esher for Readers Union

ACKNOWLEDGEMENTS

Some of the information about nineteenth-century working class scientists and naturalists is drawn from *Lancashire: The First Industrial Society* by C. Aspin (Helmshore Local History Society, 1969).

I am grateful for permission to reproduce short passages for the purposes of illustration from the following books: "The Old Dissent" by Frank Beckwith, collected in *A History of Christianity in Yorkshire*, F. S. Popham (ed.) (The Religious Education Press Ltd); *Churches and the Working Class in Victorian England* by K. S. Inglis (Routledge & Kegan Paul, 1963); and *Crimsworth Dean Methodist Chapel and Sunday School Centenary Year* by W. Stanley Greenwood. I am particularly grateful to Kenneth Young whose *Chapel* provided me with the sources of some of the stories of early Methodist conversions; and to Phyllis Bentley whose *The Pennine Weaver* provided information on the Luddites.

I must also thank Adelaide Shaw, James Nicholls, William Holt, Charles Chambers, Ernest Hall and the workers at Leigh Mills, Pudsey for their willing co-operation, and the many other people who have helped or advised with the script.

The photograph of Adelaide Shaw was presented by her to the author. Several plates are reproduced from picture postcards. The rest of the photographs were taken, and the map was drawn, by the author.

G. H.

LIST OF ILLUSTRATIONS

MILLSTONE GRIT

I AM WRITING about, I am living in, that block of the Pennines made of millstone grit, and ringed with the Yorkshire wool towns to the east and the Lancashire cotton towns to the west; those towns whose lights at night dance in little cups and hollows between peninsulas of the moors, from which they look like safe little harbours. (Or they are like the lights of ships which, with the stars, continuously puncture one dark fabric of the world and its sky.)

Beyond here are the plains—Cheshire, Lancashire and Yorkshire—where the Roman and the medieval towns were built; and the pale abbeys and churches whose delicate, ethereal stones mirror the changing lights; the plains, soaked with centuries of blood and manure, where our wars were fought and where rivers and ditches worm pink with dawns and sunsets, as if twice daily they remembered the blood of wars.

The Pennines are marked by the more recent, less frequently romanticized brutalities of the Industrial Revolution. The Romans did have camps here. But, in part, they were first thoroughly inhabited by thieves, gangsters, and murderers who hid in then inaccessible places from eighteenth-century justice; they and their sons were the ingenious men who invented so much of industry.

And a little later their steep-sided valleys were flooded (rather than inhabited) by people driven here by "events"; they were people dispossessed of their plains' heritage because they had to find work. The stones of the mills and terraces of houses that they erected are not ethereal, light and mysterious, like the stones of the medieval buildings; they are mechanical, black, and stay black through every change of light and season.

Most recently, their towns have been marked, and are still being marked, by an official vandalism. Communities are burned, and shovelled away, to be replaced by architectural abstractions; old places, with their complete identities and cultures, are turned into the ubiquitous sterility of "new towns".

There is a sense of loss. There is a feeling that wealth was made here in the nineteenth century, as it was made in more distant colonies; and that the wealth was transported to fight England's foreign wars and to establish the wealth of trading London; and there is a peevish feeling that, if life and industry are fading here, and money is needed from elsewhere to revive it, then what government money we might receive is no more than a partial paying-back of what we have given.

I was not born here; but I have stayed here for the last fifteen years. What brought me to this broken, pitted landscape that—at least sometimes, when bitter winds cross the frost; when snow is stacked upon moorland roads; when cold rain sleeks lugubrious factory walls; and when it seems an uncomfortable place where the punished old have been left to die whilst the young go adventuring— might be described as the English Siberia?

The genteel landscape of North Cheshire on to which I was born is quite flat, except for tiny hilly rises or dips into small lakes, that only my childhood imagination could transform into mountains, jungles and swamps. It is a neat well-kept place. It is beautiful—at least, it was in that childhood before selective weedkillers, when wild flowers grew in the hedgerows and butterflies drifted over them; and before the selected grass became a uniform, sterile green like paint over the land.

But it is a nondescript place. It is a place without a culture. Apart from Lord Warren de Tabley, which poets have been born there since the unknown author of *Sir Gawain and The Green Knight*? There isn't even a good football team in the county. I think it has some Conservative members of Parliament who have reached knighthoods, or cabinet positions. Lewis Carroll was born in Cheshire and so was Milton's second—or was she his third?—wife.

The county is characterized by its privacy, which first of all I invaded as a marauder; as one of a reckless gang from a housing estate. This countryside was guarded against us by a gamekeeper whom we called "Grassy". I didn't know he was a gamekeeper; I didn't know what a gamekeeper was. Grassy was a malign spirit in the woods. We feared him. I only met him once, when, just as he might set a snare on a trail he detected was used by a hare, he waited for us at the trampled gap in a fence which we plainly used for entrance and exit. He beat me on the back with a walking stick as I ran away, I being the first one he could catch up with, the slowest runner. I remember his nobbly, excessively-rural stick; his Harris tweed suit; his trousers tucked into hairy socks; and his heavy, brown, polished shoes. Remembering him now, Grassy seems very like a businessman who has bought his suit for a rural weekend.

When we invaded orchards and made dens under the thick, wax, evergreen leaves of rhododendron bushes in private woods; or when, excitedly, we hid, or we fled, as a pigeon (say) landing clumsily in a birch tree made us fear that Grassy was coming; I was searching to submerge myself completely and to become, myself, part of that green and vital growth, which seemed to be so absent from the council-house estate where I lived. From what I've learnt about the nature of religious experience, that was a religious experience—achieved only by successful combat with its particular devil, its embodiment of the forces of Evil, Grassy; and with his ministers, those other misanthropic gardeners and farmers.

On the edges of that landscape are houses and gardens built by the Victorian rich; they were the homes of those who had made fortunes out of Lancashire cotton in the nineteenth century. Each one is grandiose; intricate gardens and orchards are temptingly private behind high walls and fusty evergreens that hide the nakedness of each house, just as layers of clothing hid the bodies of Victorian men and women. At Bowdon, where there is one of the few hills overlooking the plain, these houses nudge each other like Venetian palaces. We used to raid their gardens, to eat raw vegetables where they grew, and to steal fruit. Once, I found a key in a door that led through a wall to the foot of one of these gardens. I stole it; and from then until I lost it I, myself, was master of the key to a magical land of abundance and fertility.

When I was eleven I discovered a formula that allowed me to indulge my love of nature: it was called "natural history".

As part of a radio programme of that time called *Children's Hour* there was a regular fifteen minute piece called "Out with Romany". Romany, as I remember him, was an educated gypsy—a glamorous Lady Chatterley's lover, without the fornication—who befriended two children at a farm at which he camped; episode by episode, as the seasons revealed themselves, he educated the children in the half-secret life of English hedgerows.

After a little good-tempered banter, BBC Sound Effects would produce the tinny sound of a tiny bird.

"Why, that's a sparrow!" one of the children exclaimed, with excessive delight and curiosity.

"Ah, yes; a sparrow. But what kind of sparrow?" asked Romany, the perfect teacher.

"Do you mean there's more than one kind of sparrow, Romany?"

"Oh, yes, there's the tree sparrow, that wears a little black cap— you see his little black cap, much brighter than the common house sparrow as it's called? Then there's the hedge sparrow, which has a much sweeter song. Why, there's one singing its chirpy melody right now amongst those blackthorns. Do you hear him?" (Sound of hedge sparrow, singing.) "But he's not really a member of the sparrow family at all. He's a misnomer . . ."

If we were being taught about plants, that didn't make sounds, Romany's eloquence became more descriptive. I was devoted to that fifteen minutes of radio.

One day, amongst the rudimentary crossword puzzles and the quasi Enid Blyton stories of the "Children's Corner" of the local paper, there was an advertisement for a "Romany Society" and the name and address of a local secretary. The first meeting was to be on Sunday morning, outside Altrincham railway station, from which the society was to take a train to Knutsford, ten miles away, and "go on a nature ramble".

Romany Society meetings being on Sunday mornings made them more attractive to me because usually on that morning I was sent to church to wear cassock and surplice and sing in the choir. My Aunt Liza, who went to a Methodist church occasionally, thought that to wander around muddy fields with a strange man would be a diabolical change from going to church; my father opined that God was as much manifested in the hedgerows as he was in church (he was a great talker, was my dad, as everybody said); and my mother, who knew that I was rebelling against the church routine anyway—I often had stomach ache and a dizzy head on Sunday morning—followed the necessary will of things, and adventurously and gladly took me to Altrincham railway station on the next Sunday morning.

We met Mr Murdoch. He was dressed in rural tweeds, just like Grassy. He was leaning on a folded golfing umbrella—a huge black and green thing, like a garden party tent, I discovered when he opened it later in the day. He also carried a big black tin on a leather strap; and a rucksack. There were three other boys, each one about my age, waiting with him; one of them was his son. Mr Murdoch chatted to my mother, but not much to me; and she seemed to trust him, although he was without such institutional authority as doctors and teachers and clergymen have. He told my mother that he had a newsagent's business.

As soon as we walked along the first hedgerow out of Knutsford, I expected nature to reveal herself; and that then explanations would come, as they did in Romany broadcasts. Mr Murdoch, who was wearing Army boots, had a peculiarly vigorous walk; it would have been difficult to keep up with him, if he had not every ten minutes or so brought from his pocket an Ordnance Survey map, and spent time looking at it. Also, he paused, abrupt and intense, before patches of hedge or bankside, and spoke to them in Latin.

"*Achilea millifolium!*" he said, to something invisible from me in

the grass. He spoke as if he were making indelible marks with his
words.

Very early on in that momentous walk, when I and the two
boys who were not his sons were hanging back, out of nervousness,
about twenty yards behind Mr Murdoch, he became very excited,
and waved his golfing umbrella in the air. A big, grey bird lifted
clumsily from behind a hedge, buckling its wings awkwardly;
gaining a little height, it sailed gracefully away.

"A heron!" he shouted. Hopeful of watching it further out of
sight, he ran across the ploughed field, the edge of which we were
carefully treading. He stopped part way to wave to us boys. "Come
on! Come on!" he shouted, waving his umbrella and his head, so
that his glasses sparkled in the sunlight. Then he turned and ran to
the boundary hedge.

When we caught up with him, the heron had gone. He told us
that, had we not been chattering loudly, but had instead silently
walked in a special way that he showed us—putting our feet down
toes first (I don't know how he did it, in Army boots), feeling for
any sticks that might crackle noisily under foot, and then following
with the heel after sensing that we were not going to make a noise
—we might have got very close to where the heron fished in a
tiny pond. He told us this without the slightest air of grumbling—
which I remember gratefully, for it was so different from the way
my teachers would have told me.

When we stopped in a little wood, and Mr Murdoch ate salad
sandwiches and drank cold tea, I felt that I'd never been so happy in
my life.

Every now and then, Mr Murdoch—very delicately, very girl-
ishly—picked a plant from this wayside green that was now revealing
itself as a rich jungle of a multitude of unidentified forms, and put
the plant in his tin box, which he called a "vasculum".

Sometimes he would pick a plant, and after fingering its leaves
and counting its petals, he would say, for instance, "A member of
the *Cruciferae* family. They all have four petals, like a cross. Let's
find out what it's called." He would open his rucksack, and bring

out a dark little book with pictures of flowers in it. The book, he said, was not a book: it was a flora. He himself was learning the names of birds, plants, and insects; the ones for which he knew an English name, he was learning a Latin one.

During the following week I could not wait for the arrival of Sunday, when I went to Altrincham railway station with a rucksack holding salad sandwiches and a flask of cold tea. None of the other boys, excepting, of course, Mr Murdoch's son, turned up. This day, we went on a ramble to Delamere Forest. Sunday after Sunday, he took me on similar walks.

Mr Murdoch was one of the few good teachers I have met. Whilst showing me the intricate lacings of footpaths over the Cheshire countryside, he taught me to read a map; and to identify birds, animals, insects and plants—and a little Latin, in consequence of that. He taught me to take, develop, and print photographs. Also, as Mr Murdoch wrote long Augustan poems in the manner of James Thompson about our walks and published them in the local paper, so I, too, read and wrote poetry, for very much the same reason that I drank cold tea and ate salad sandwiches on our rambles.

I had only vague hints—for instance, from the slight, unnecessary smiles of farmers whom we met sometimes—that there was something eccentric about this man. And only very much later have I realized that there is a question to ask about the existence of an uneducated man with a passion for learning, with a knowledge of Latin, and who wrote quasi-Augustan poems; and that the answer to that question lies in a peculiarly northern, working-class tradition of people like him, which was bred during the Industrial Revolution in Lancashire and Yorkshire.

Karl Marx wrote that the one good he could find in the Industrial Revolution was that it released the working class from what he called "the idiocy of rural life". Those hordes of agricultural workers, Irish immigrants, and soldiers demobilized from the Napoleonic wars, who came to Lancashire and Yorkshire to learn to weave and to earn (for a short while) high wages, developed an extraordinary consciousness of both the awfulness of their condition and of the cultural inheritance of which they were dispossessed. During that frightfulness of the nineteenth century in Lancashire and Yorkshire, the Chartists and the Luddites and the creators of the Co-Operative movement and of the trade unions, who fashioned the first political consciousness of the working class; the non-conformist preachers who had the energy to walk over the moors to preach sometimes twenty or thirty times a week to congregations who had sometimes walked twenty miles to hear them; the "model employers" who built schools and libraries and who worked for factory legislation; and, maybe rather peculiarly, the very large movement of working-class mathematicians, scientists, inventors, and naturalists, are signs of extraordinary intellectual activity within appalling conditions.

John Butterworth, of Haggate, Oldham, born in 1774, who became a jenny spinner at the age of six, who was twenty before he could read and write well, who for most of his life was a fustian weaver, but who by 1840 was running his own little school, and who was a contributor to the leading mathematical journals of the day; the factory worker of Rochdale, who (as it was discovered by a factory inspector in 1836) was so fond of classical learning that he had named his children Xanthippe, Diaphantes, and Pandora Barraclough; the Manchester botanist, James Crowther, born in a cellar in 1768, son of a labourer, who began work as a drawboy at petticoat weaving, and who after a day's work would sometimes walk twenty miles to collect a specimen of a plant; and John Horsefield, of Besses o' The Barn, near Manchester, who learned the Latin names of plants from lists pinned to the post of his handloom, were the ancestors of Mr Murdoch.

These men gave rise to those weighty literary institutes, lyceums, mechanics' institutes, literary and philosophical societies and temperance societies in most Lancashire and Yorkshire towns—like the Royton Temperance Society, founded by a group of young starving workpeople to discover ways of educating themselves during the riots of 1842, and who built their own premises, with a library, maps, a globe, and an organ; or the Oldham Botanical Society, whose members paid 2d. per month for books and 4d. a month for drink, and by 1795 had twenty books and 1,500 plant specimens (one of its members "had undertaken a voyage as far as the western parts of America to botanize under the patronage of John Lee Philips of Manchester",[1] according to a contemporary agriculturist, John Hall).

They were not small gatherings; their success was extraordinary. For instance, at the first public lecture at the Manchester Institute, when the Rev. Andrew Wilson spoke on "Mechanical Philosophy" "long before the appointed time every avenue to the theatre was completely blocked up, and when the doors were opened, a tremendous rush took place, and in a very few minutes the building was crowded to excess"[2] with 1,400 people; whilst the same number had to be turned away.

These men were as inventive in the cause of culture as they were in creating industrial technology. The directors of the Warrington Mechanics' Institute, for instance, in order to increase borrowings from their library, bought a one-horse van, filled it with books and sent it once a week to "every door in Warrington and the vicinity",[3] thus increasing book borrowings from 3,000 to 12,000 books a year.

This vigorous tradition was behind Mr Murdoch and made him, after all, not a lonely, eccentric figure. Mr Murdoch's sentiments were the same as those of Richard Buxton, the Manchester botanist who, when he was over sixty years old, regularly walked thirty miles in a day to look for plant specimens, and who, when introducing his book on the plant life around Manchester, wrote, in 1849, "fields and woods, although the rich man's heritage, may still be the poor man's flower garden".[4]

[1] C. Aspin, *Lancashire: The First Industrial Society*, Helmshore Local History Society, 1969.
[2] Ibid.   [3] Ibid.   [4] Ibid.

Mr Murdoch, leading me through the Cheshire countryside, trespassing across fields to discover plants and birds, had the same determination as the Manchester naturalist James Crowther, who "notwithstanding all his precautions, was often pursued and had many narrow escapes from being captured. He often contrived to elude his pursuers by his extraordinary swiftness in running. Many were the chases he had, but the most severe was with Mr Hopwood's keepers in Hopwood Park. They once pursued him three or four miles across the country without stopping and he considered it nearly a miracle that he escaped them."[1]

Mr Murdoch was one of the working-class scientists and naturalists whom Mrs Gaskell described in *Mary Barton*:

There is a class of men in Manchester, unknown even to many of the inhabitants, and whose existence will probably be doubted by many, who yet may claim kindred with all the noble names that science recognizes. I said "in Manchester" but they are scattered all over the manufacturing districts of Lancashire. In the neighbourhood of Oldham there are weavers, common hand-loom weavers, who throw the shuttle with unceasing sound, though Newton's "Principia" lies open upon the loom, to be snatched at in work hours, but revelled over in meal times or at night. Mathematical problems are received with interest and studied with absorbing attention by many a broad-spoken, common-looking factory hand. It is perhaps less astonishing that the more popularly interesting branches of natural history have their warm and devoted followers among this class. There are botanists among them, equally familiar with either the Linnaean or the Natural system, who know the name and habitat of every plant within a day's walk from their dwellings; who steal the holiday of a day or two when any particular plant should be in flower, and tying up their simple food in their pocket handkerchiefs, set off with single purpose to fetch home the humble-looking weed. There are entomologists who may be seen with

[1] Ibid.

a rude-looking net, ready to catch any winged insect, or a kind of dredge with which they rake the green and slimy pools; practical, shrewd, hard-working men, who pore over every new specimen with real scientific delight.

Mrs Gaskell wrote of someone whom I knew, and who taught me; of a kind like Mr Murdoch, or in a different way like my father; a type of man who has influenced my life many times, and of whom I will have to write several times in this book.

In contrast to that eighteenth-century landscape of huge parks and estate farms that swept in most of the country within reach of my childhood explorations was the council-house estate (despised and just a little feared for its unpredictable roughness by the county bourgeoisie) where my father, unaided and alone, and with a strength of will greater, I think, than I could ever summon, discovered and cultivated literature as both an escape from, and a measure of, his life that was made reflective and meditative by his experience as an out-of-work lad in the 1920s. The novels of H. G. Wells and the tracts of Bernard Shaw, Bertrand Russell, and the Webbs, were stacked above a cupboard and in and around an inadequate bookcase.

My father was a bus conductor who was given a timely promotion to the salaried post of ticket inspector to lift him out of union activities that threatened his employers. When he was working a late shift he would spend the morning reading those books whilst I was at school and my mother was cleaning other people's houses. He would stay up half the night to read. If I woke in the night, it might be because he was throwing coal on to the fire. If I woke without disturbance, sensing that the night silence was pregnant with his activities, and to find out what he was doing went downstairs with the excuse that I needed the lavatory, I would pass him, with his feet on the grate, reading *The New Machiavelli* or *The World of William Clissold*. Sometimes he would then keep me from my bed, to talk to me of Wells and of Shaw; it was thus that I learnt to revere books and idolize the occupation of writer that seemed, in those circumstances, magically creative and godlike.

Literature at school was nothing. I could not cope with it. It had nothing to do with my life or with the life of anyone whom I loved. It was a mess of words laid on a desk for analyses that I felt incompetent to practice. I felt only frustration that led to positive distaste that made me almost determine to fail at answering questions on set books, at doing précis, at analysing sentences and thoughts.

Between the two spheres, of my father's Fabian literature and of the books at school (the titles of which I have forgotten—I guess they were various "golden" anthologies, snippets of poems and prose) I felt that I had to discover books of my own.

I went into the public library first of all because Dad sent me to get a "good" book for him. Feeling resentful, I would pull any book from the shelf and take it back to him. He always read what I brought, I think—all printed words had authority and potency. Eventually, when I was about thirteen years old, I discovered a writer of my own on those public library shelves.

It was Richard Jefferies. When I read him, I felt closer to him than to anyone I knew personally: closer to him than I was to boys and girls on the housing estate, to teachers and to other adults, certainly; and closer, perhaps, than I felt to my mother and my father.

Richard Jefferies was dead: so it was a kind of magic, this kinship through his remains.

I changed my handwriting to imitate his scrawl that I discovered from a biography containing a holograph (for the first time in many years I have just taken that book from my shelves, and discovered how similar my handwriting still is to his); I parted my hair in the centre of my forehead and even, I think, developed that inward look of his eyes as they are romantically portrayed in the photograph of the bust of him which I had not seen in the National Portrait Gallery.

It was Richard Jefferies, my adopted, unfleshed friend, who taught me to have emotions about hills, sparse grass, the climbing of slopes, and the particular space of hills, before I had ever seen a hill. Childhood maraudings, which led me to literature, eventually brought me to the Pennine hills.

Richard Jefferies wrote what he called an "Autobiography", *The Story of My Heart* (a rather sick, self-indulgent book, I suspect; but I cannot judge it and I avoid rereading it for the same reason that one doesn't trust revisiting places of former happiness). It contains sentences of pantheistic adoration of hills:

There was a hill to which I used to resort at such periods. The labour of walking three miles to it, all the while gradually ascending, seemed to clear my blood of the heaviness accumulated at home. On a warm summer day the slow continued rise required continual effort, which carried away the sense of oppression. The familiar everyday scene was out of sight; I came to other trees, meadows, and fields; I began to breathe a new air and have a fresher inspiration. I restrained my soul until I reached the sward of the hill. . . .

Moving up the sweet short turf, at every step my heart seemed to obtain a wider horizon of feeling; with every inhalation of rich pure air, a deeper desire. The very light of the sun was whiter and more brilliant here. By the time I had reached the summit I had entirely forgotten the petty circumstances and the annoyance of existence. I felt myself, myself.

When I was thirteen years old I practised these spiritual exercises as I climbed the pathetic little knoll in Dunham Park. I became overwhelmingly interested in the mysteries of this feeling before nature, and it eclipsed my interest in the details of identifying nature's manifestations. Scientific natural history had become banal; I became a pantheist.

I was now emotionally prepared for the time when my father discovered a new way of spending Sunday. Because he was a ticket inspector, he could travel free of charge on bus services. He began to make a Sunday hobby of taking me on buses for distances of up to thirty miles from our house, and going for walks either at our destination or between bus routes on the way. He was proud of being able to stop a bus anywhere, with a wave of his hand, as one stops a taxi; and of his knowledge of the timing and routing of every small bus service.

On one of these excursions he took me twenty-five miles, to the moors above Buxton, Derbyshire.

The bus climbed a hill steeper and longer than any I had seen before, through Buxton suburbs that slowly broke into gaps for fields followed by scattered farms and fields chained in stone walls.

We left the bus at a high point of the moors, the Cat and Fiddle Inn—the highest pub in England, I remember him telling me. The emotion that I felt when I looked over those grey, round hills slinking through the mist and saw, for the first time, stone farms below me (as if I were a flying bird); and rushes; and sparse grass; and the tiny waterfalls of the Goyt Valley stumbling through red bracken and grey rocks, is still with me now as I write, as one of the most powerful emotions of my life, like the emotion of first making love. We had travelled only twenty-five miles; but no two places could be more different than the countryside south of Manchester and these millstone-grit hills.

Moving to live in the Pennine hills, when I was old enough to build foundations for my independent life, was a move towards fulfilling those childhood emotions. A prime need of my life came to be a need for the clarity, the airiness, and the space that I associated with hills.

But to find such things unadulterated on the Pennine hills meant deluding myself. It meant blotting from my senses the characteristics that are quite special to these hills, as to nowhere else in the British Isles except, maybe, South Wales; and I blotted them out because they adulterated the vision, the embodiment of which I sought.

The Pennine moors often have an intoxicatingly powerful beauty. On foggy days in the towns, the moors rise above the fog, and because the more usual obscurities of the air have sunk into the valleys, the hills' sunlit colours are brilliant, and distant objects have a startling clarity, the hills an archipelago of islands in the wandering fog. In March, when the old grass, whinberry and heather are burnt so that their ashes might fertilize new growth (they call it "sweeling") whole hills are dramatically on fire; and in autumn the hills are turned the duller, more resonant red of the decaying herbage. In late summer, the sunlight strikes purple heather mixed with white grass.

One day, I walked on the Pennine moors and ran my fingers along a blade of grass. Each finger was marked by two black lines of soot.

I wiped my fingers and ran them along another blade of grass on these empty moors where one can walk almost twenty miles without seeing a farmhouse, let alone a town or village; and my fingers were again marked.

On other still summer days I have lain in hollows in the remotest places and listened intently through what was, apparently, silence; and distinguished, beside the song of a lark or the call of a grouse, a continuous hum so constant, monotonous and quiet that I had mistaken it for silence; and realized that it was the day and night unceasing noises of Lancashire and Yorkshire, as constant, incessant and inevitable as the flow of a river.

I have walked through this empty, spacious landscape, and realized that it is a derelict one.

The paradox of this countryside is that, from the densities of old industrial towns, you may turn a corner or climb a hill, and be in a world that seems pristine, and utterly untouched, like a world before creation. The soft, ever-changing light; the ever-shifting peat bogs that are as formless as putty; the lifeless earth and air; and the lack of human activity, seem like the soft and shapeless mass of the earth before anything was created upon it.

In fact, it isn't. In fact, it's as much a ruin as the towns. From the sixteenth century onwards, the inhabitants of the fringe of this moorland have been without much interest in a land so difficult to farm; they turned their interest to the weaving of cloth, and to the industrialization of that weaving—that was something that the regular, soft water made easy to do. When, in the eighteenth century, they began to build those "intake" farms—so-called because they were little attacks to "take in" bits of the sterile, inhibiting moorland—his little farm was only part of the farmer's necessity; his attention was only half-focused upon it. What else could it do for him, besides maybe support a pig or a cow; or, if it was sufficiently far down the hillside to have a little soil covering the rocks, grow a little corn and a few vegetables?

That was not enough. For the real substance of his life, he bought raw wool. After spreading it on hurdles, or over his cottage floor, he beat it with sticks; picked out obvious impurities; and treated it with oil, or with home-made butter. Then his children carded it—that is, they stroked it with something like a hair brush set with iron spikes—to work it into a froth. His own women— or, as it took half a dozen spinners to keep one weaver working, some of the widows and unmarried women ("spinsters") of the district—spun it. The spun wool was dipped in the stream to soften it for weaving; then it was dried by swinging it in a basket hung on a stick. The farmer spent most of his daylight hours weaving. After a piece was woven, he spread it on the floor and the family trampled the piece in human or animal waste and urine, to take the grease out of the cloth (but later on soda-ash was used for this); then he took the piece on a donkey's back to the fulling mill, where it was beaten with wooden hammers driven by water power, so that the fibres clung together, and the wool was thickened. Then the weaver brought his piece home again and stretched it on a frame in the open air, called a "tenter"; afterwards he took his piece to be finished by cropping the nap of the wool in a "cropping shed", and to be made-up into material lengths.

For all this to-ing and fro-ing with hanks of wool, innumerable stony pack-horse roads were built over the hills; then canals, which were rather wonderful because of the number of pack-horse loads that could be carried on one barge.

In the nineteenth century, one ingenious method after another was invented to industrialize these processes; and with no one knows what suffering, the farmer who had never really been dedicated to his scrap of unco-operative moor became a servant to a powerful, ruthless man; and then to a company of such men. Tides of smoke crossed the hills and helped the weather to dwindle the growth.

What had all those lives to do with care for the land? So when you see old farmhouses, large or small, on the hills, they do not look as you expect farmhouses to look. They lack that air of abundant, teeming life; of the centuries of manure, producing abundance; of the movements of animals and the carting of hay and of crops deciding the ways over the hills. They are dour, and black, and bleak; and so like the little mills they actually were, with men and women processing wool in their rooms.

In some of the most unlikely places, in some of its most bleak and rocky places, as on the plateau of Saddleworth Moor, black gnarled pieces of tree-root, at sight hardly distinguishable from rock, are embedded or half embedded in the sour peat. There was once a forest there. That bleak place, thinly covered by a matted hair of grey-yellow grass, its smooth featureless outline marked only by the small eruptions of unsuccessful nineteenth-century coal mining, ice-age boulders and the boulders laid aside after quarrying, unnatural sheets of water and the Gothic turrets of the Water Board and the old railway company, is still called Denshaw Forest. On the moors there are mounds, squared-off dykes, low humps of grassed-over stones, looking as ancient as Celtic forts, that are the remains of farmhouses and buildings that have sunk into the ground within living memory—in one form or another, the dereliction of this land, so close to huge masses of people, has gone on for centuries and it still continues. Laboriously built walls, now broken down by sheep, ice and hikers, divide the hills into small spaces so that you realize they were once important, though now one space of rushes and bog is indistinguishable from another: they were grazing areas, or even fields of tilled earth, the grass and some basic subsistence crops for humans and animals and poultry preciously cultivated against late springs, cool damp summers, and early, vicious winters. This hilly place between two packed industrial areas is a man-made desert.

But deserts, though many are actually monuments to man's destruction of the natural world, have a peculiar attraction for the human psyche, projecting as they do the huge spaciousness that we each feel our soul to be.

As I matured and discovered the fatalities that continuously threaten mortal life—war, sickness, failure, poverty and guilt— maybe this desert had a particular grip upon me because its arraignment against poisonous, dirty and ugly towns destructive of the human spirit, is a symbol of the human condition, balanced between the impulses of inspiration and destruction.

And I think it is more than an arbitrary accident that when preindustrial artists painted their images of Hell—I am thinking of Bosch and of Breughel—their flaming wastes amongst dark, amorphous, threatening forms bear the most striking resemblance to the industrial valleys of Lancashire and West Yorkshire, Huddersfield, Colne, Rochdale, Burnley, Oldham, that were to make the painters' horrifying visions into palpable realities.

2

THE STONE, THAT you see bonily sticking out of the landscape everywhere you look, as the bones press through the flesh of a hungry cow, is black.

It doesn't need sooty air to turn millstone grit black. The cleanest air will oxidize it from its lovely orange and gold, as you see it when it first bursts open, sparkling with innumerable glassy crystals of silica, to the black, black, that makes your eyes ache everywhere in West Yorkshire, so that you think of dirt, no matter how clean and bright the day.

It is this stone that defines the area of which I write. Northwards, the millstone grit ends at the Aire Gap; beyond it are the limestone hills of the Yorkshire Dales. Southwards, beyond Chapel-en-le-Frith, is the limestone of Derbyshire. Driving north or driving south, you notice, a mile or so before the geology changes, that the black millstone-grit walls have increasing numbers of white stones in them, which have drifted out of the limestone—presumably from wall to wall, from hand to hand. Then there is a sudden change. There are no more bleak cotton or wool-processing mill towns, because they depend upon the rainwater thrown off millstone grit, in rivers and in streams; whereas limestone soaks the water into itself, carrying it in underground streams, where it riddles the rocks with caves, like the tunnels in a sponge. The limestone slopes are more gentle, and the land pastoral, and scribbled over with trees, as if with careless handwriting.

And east and west the land drops into the earthy plains, Yorkshire and Lancashire.

I'm sure that this geology has defined, also, the general temperament of the people upon it. The geology made possible the mills; therefore it gave the place its social history; and that—apart from any more mysterious influence of the environment—has made the customs, the relationships, the ways of speaking of the inhabitants. Briefly, they are usually described as "dour".

As in my home at Millbank, Sowerby Bridge, for instance.

Millbank is a hamlet of seventy houses, built above the crossing place of a stream that is a tributary of a tributary of the River Calder—the River Calder is the most useful river in the district, so its valleys hold most of the factories and habitations.

Almost every stream in East Lancashire and West Yorkshire has villages and hamlets similar to Millbank on its banks; villages which are neither rural nor industrial, whose black stones without gardens cluster together in the misty spaces, and sometimes seem to hang in the air, so that they are like swarms of dark flies.

People lived there when the valleys were marshes and the roads kept to the flanks of the hills, where they were neither so high that they would be exposed to violent weather, nor so low that they would be bogged down. Most of these villages are the tiny, dwindling, parent villages of big industrial towns in the valleys—as Sowerby is to Sowerby Bridge, as Luddenden is to Luddenden Foot, and as Heptonstall is to Hebden Bridge.

Millbank developed organically for several centuries, very slowly, around a twelfth-century corn mill on the old pack-horse route from Yorkshire to Lancashire, where the road crossed the stream; then, in the nineteenth century, it grew more quickly, when the slopes of the hillside that were too rough for cattle grazing were used to house workers in the commercial boom.

The result was a picturesque, closely-packed group, where no stone had been placed without a reason.

But about the year 1965 it had finished its history, it seemed.

The local council began to demolish houses that were unwanted when they became empty. It thereby created ugly stone and weed-strewn gaps that became communal rubbish dumps overlooked by the shattered interior walls that were now exterior walls of a neighbouring house.

Wallpapers flapped like bats' wings until the rain peeled them and the wind blew them about the village; and the sight of those walls, with their fireplaces fixed surrealistically half-way up, and with their insights into once-hidden bedrooms, was as embarrassing as glimpses of someone's underwear.

So, like many of the cottages when I strayed into this desolate village, as it was in 1970, my house was boarded up.

The neighbours told me who owned it. It belonged to a local mill, which had bought it for one of their lorry-drivers who needed a house in a hurry; after a few years he and his wife moved to something that he thought was better and left the house on the hands of its owner.

The cottage had a closure order upon it—which meant that no one could now live in it unless certain improvements were made. Nevertheless, I went to see the manager of the mill; I asked him if he'd sell the house and might I look through it?

Before he answered he stared at me slowly: searching my appearance for something as ludicrous as this request, no doubt. I had a beard; so maybe my potty request was genuine.

"Yer can look it over if you like," he said; "but yer'll not want it. Council's planning demolishing of it."

"I'd like to see it," I said. I felt as foolish as he thought me to be. I stared at his scratched filing cabinet and at his girlie calendar.

"It's boarded up, isn't it?" he asked.

"I'll nail it up again," I replied.

"You can look it over if you like. But ya'll not want it." He was very genial.

I went back to the house in Millbank. I took a hammer and pincers and pulled out the six-inch nails that held the front door.

Dressed in a mackintosh and slippers, an old woman came out of a nearby house and put pieces of bread on the road for the birds, where they would probably get run over whilst they were eating. Either she thought that even a bird shouldn't enter the Everlasting Kingdom unfed; or it was an excuse to come out and look at me. I found out later that the newspapers had made people nervous here. There was a theory about what was happening to Millbank. It was: "These hippies are taking over." The "hippies" are half a dozen people who have longish hair and beards, wear ex-military combat clothes, are rather more articulate than the average villager, and are either in the village, like lay-abouts, during the day; or are absent from the village for days and weeks at a stretch, at times other than Christmas and the annual Wakes holiday. Confused with the hippies are a few school-teachers who look a bit artistic, and who live in houses with bare boards.

Another woman amongst an uncountable flock of children stopped in the street and looked at me severely, as though she were a policeman; so I told her what I was doing.

"Nobody's lived there for about seven years," she said, quietly, melancholy, her voice trailing off into a dying fall; "Somebody broke in and pinched all the water pipes. They took the 'lectric wiring as well. You can't leave anything these days."

There were some letters behind the door that rain following them through the letter box had unstuck. They were electricity bills, all for the same quarter, those of the latest date being printed in red; and there were some other threatening letters to do with money.

There wasn't a smell of damp. I pulled a plank from the down-stairs window to let in the light. There was an untidy mess of news-papers over a stone floor. Where this had been most walked on for a hundred years, a pool of water had formed. Behind this room was a very small room without any windows at all. It smelled of urine; and it was fitted with a porcelain sink, so it was a kitchen, evidently. There was a wooden partition at the end of it, with a wooden door that was nailed up; I didn't bother to open that.

The woman, and some of the children, had followed me in. "That'll be the coal 'ole," she said.

So the coal was shot straight from the street beyond the house into the windowless kitchen, with nothing but a bit of wood to hold it back!

I climbed some foot-worn stone stairs to the upper room—there was only one. The floorboards were sound, except for one place where the wood was damp, and shredded into soft woolly splinters, the way a pair of tweed trousers go when they are about to fray into a hole. The ceiling was sound, except for a hole in the plaster above the bad place in the floorboards. I imagined a hole in the roof.

I nailed the door up again. The house had a cellar, which was reached only by a door from the street, and I didn't look in there because it was silted up with rubbish.

I went back to the mill manager.

"There's no electricity nor water in there," I said—I'd heard how cheap houses were in Millbank, and I didn't want to offer very much.

"That's reet."

"The floorboards are rotten. It needs new window frames. I'll offer you fifty pounds."

"Reet," he said.

When I had bought my house I went back to find out a little more about it.

It was built "back to back"—and a little bit "back to earth", as well. That is, the houses at the back of and at the side of mine have rooms or parts of rooms that run over or under some of my rooms, like an interlocking puzzle. In this, it is typical of many houses in the village. There are, for instance, two cottages built under a mill. The whole building is built into the slope of the hill, so that though from the road side the cottages are subterranean, on the other side both of their two storeys face into the air—that's "back to earth". This interlocking in fact makes them very snug—though doubtless cheapness had something to do with their being built that way.

Many of the houses are like warrens, in blocks that have an immense, heartless grandeur—blocks of houses that are only a little less grand than the Methodist Chapel that was built, with

c

heavy-handed symbolism, at the crown, the highest point, of the village. When you look at the village from across the valley, you see a pyramid of undistinguished black stone, its peak being the two Italianate turrets of the chapel spiking the sky.

As soon as I began to live here I discovered the disadvantage of this interlocking.

A bathroom for a neighbouring house had been built above the ceiling of my bedroom. There's no record in my house-deeds of a bathroom suspended over the bedroom; apparently whoever built it simply trespassed with it. Neither my neighbour; nor her land-lady; nor a woman who lived there before either of these two; nor an old man who used to live in my cellar when it was what was called a "cellar cottage"—a single, subterranean room—remember the bathroom being built. It was, it would seem, "always" there.

It hung, threateningly, over my bed. The waste pipe from the bath and the lavatory crossed my ceiling to a pipe on the outside wall. As I lay in bed I heard the waste sliding, glug, glug, down the pipe: it took ten minutes to cross my ceiling. The outside pipe had a little decorative top to it, like lace, but made of iron. The inside waste pipe was about a foot thick, and made of lead. The lead was maybe worth nearly as much as I'd paid for the cottage.

Another trouble was that sound travelled so easily through the partitions that separated our homes, that my neighbour and I knew as much about one another as a man knows about his wife, and a wife knows about her husband.

It wasn't merely a muffled impression of sound that we heard. It was a daylong, nightlong, anatomy of sounds—the sound-skeletons of our lives, without the flesh of sights, conversations, and mutually significant happenings: the creaking of my bed; the scratchings, slammings, sweeping of the stairs, and conversations with her neighbours, that were the material through which I thought I understood her life.

There are two roads through Millbank. Upper Millbank Road

holds the bus stop; the telephone kiosk; the school, with over its door the motto that no one can understand, DEO ECCLESIA PAUPERIBUS AD 1850; the rickety, wooden, untenanted butcher's shop, perched unsteadily upon its stones, temporary-looking, like a gull upon a rock; the chapel and the Methodist School, turned into homes, the Working-Men's Club, turned into a home; and the still used post office, where you can buy bread, and coal, and corn-plasters, and remedies for rheumatism. Lower Millbank Road, where I live, is without any public buildings. So I suppose Upper Millbank Road is our main thoroughfare, although both roads disperse themselves, beyond woods and done-up cottages and wire-carrying poles, into the bleak countryside.

Though the terraced houses are small, they are oppressive, made of large, mechanically-cut stones with predominant pointing.

They are on one side of the road. Opposite to them is a conflicting landscape: a slope of flowery, cattle-grazed meadow falls to a stream that has trout in it—there are flashes of white as the water falls around a boulder. From the far bank of the stream the land rises through woodlands in which the horse-riders trot, the birds sing at dawn and sunset, and the owls cry at night—which sighs mysteriously in the rain and drifts through a spectrum of colours on a sunny day—to sparse fields that fade out, as a beach fades into the sea, into a mysterious space: grey and silver hills and valleys seem constantly to be changing places with similarly-shaped clouds.

For we are in the country—though what kind of country is another matter. Showing their neglect, the fields bristle with stalky weeds.

At the foot of the woods is a mill that is not derelict. Many of the woollen mills that survived the second world war did it either by changing their production to something quite different, the closest to the traditional product being that of man-made fibres; or by manufacturing very high quality, expensive woollens that, with refined and aggressive salesmanship, can survive on a small market. This mill, Blackburne and Sutcliffe, did it by changing to the dying of Terylene: but Blackburne and Sutcliffe is in the next village. At night, their mill is lit like a liner at sea amongst the dark moors; and amongst the hootings of the owls it screams irregularly, like an animal in distress.

The only thing to block the view on that side of the road is a tiny building built as solidly as the houses: stone walls with a heavy stone roof, the building not much bigger than its four padlocked doors. This is a unit of four lavatories, each one shared between two neighbours. We lock them because, although the north is, as everyone knows, very friendly and neighbourly, and we all talk about one another, we don't trust anyone not to use our lavatories or steal our toilet paper. "Good fences make good neighbours", as Robert Frost wrote.

But that is on the other side of the road. On this side, where the houses are, the country has no influence: it is as if it didn't exist. By the houses, there is no grass, no trees, no flowers growing wild in crannies of the stones, nor growing cultivated, not even in pots and window boxes. (But there is one exception. On the stone platform before his door, Mr Alderson, who once rented a little garden but lost it in recent wars of property speculation, grows, in polystyrene urns—"they're as light as a feather but they look grand" —the few peonies and chrysanthemums that he has salvaged.) There are broken iron railings leading to ugly doors, the width of the steps being the only space between the house wall and the street, and no pavement—just enough space to hold a dustbin. (In fact, not quite enough space. Sometimes a car, or more often a drunk, kicks a dustbin over into the street. It's very funny, he thinks.)

Until the building and repairing enthusiasm that came with General Improvement Grants, Millbank had the depressed atmosphere that one would expect in a conglomeration of such houses.

Throughout its day it had spasms of life, like the sporadic jerkings of a dying animal.

During the hour before 8 a.m. a few cars and vans would start— many with difficulty, for many of them were old—and leave the

village; and a few pairs of boots and clogs (which are still worn
here—there are two clog-makers in Halifax, which is seven miles
away) slurred over the road, up the stone stairs leading from Lower
Millbank Road to the top road, or over the cobblestones that still
remain by the tiny, and now unused, Methodist graveyard.

During the hour before nine o'clock in the morning, a few pretty
girls moved with hasty vitality to the village centre—that is, the bus
stop, where people had to linger no matter how cold and wet it was,
therefore they talked and looked about them. The only people who
regularly *came* here were the few teachers for the village school.

Then—unless there was a crisis, like the school kids being on
holiday; or someone from the Calderdale Water Board blowing
a whistle as he circuited the village, to tell us that it wouldn't be
possible to draw water for an hour or two because they were
working on the supply (which often happened, particularly when
they began work on house conversions); or the officers of the
Borough Council, or the architects responsible for developing the
village, coming to visit us (which they occasionally did, creating
through the rumours of their impending visit the fearful, pregnant
atmosphere that precedes pogroms and liquidations)—unless something of this kind happened, the village was silent and immobile
until midday.

Some old woman might watch through lace curtains, like an
animal hiding in a bush; or she might come out to scrub the pavement and her doorstep, in the way that only old people do it now. I
have seen old women, who have nothing to do but fill their day as
best they can by contriving breaks in the monotony, come out to
scrub the pavement at half past six in the morning, because it would
seem to them like a slovenly collapse of their lives, presaging death
and decay, to break the habit of rising early to begin work at the
mill; to break the monotony of a long morning in a room dull with
cleanliness and the tidiness of sacrosanct objects, one might clutch
a dark scarf over her head and around her throat, as if it were too
small to wrap her as she wished it to, as if she would be far more
at ease with an old-fashioned shawl, and come out to ghost through

the village at ten o'clock in the morning, on her way to the post office where she would spend half an hour (or an hour if she were lucky, and there were not too many interrupting visitors around the counter) buying groceries, or a prophylactic, or a stamp.

Or a forlorn salesman, who had already combed the housing estates, went from door to door. Though there wasn't much money here, there were people easily seduced by glittering, impermanent gadgets, and by trinkets to display, with their most attractive aspects turned to the street, on crowded window bottoms.

Or the scrap-dealer; or the pop cart; or the milkman; or the postman; or the TV rental firm made their visit.

At midday men who worked for the council parked their cleansing or hauling or digging machines in the secret lanes, and had lunch in their cabs, and an after-dinner snooze and a read of the *Daily Mirror*—they came to a quiet place to lengthen their lunch hours away from tell-tales and passing officials. Or men with a right to lengthy lunch hours dashed menacingly through Millbank in cars sprayed the washed-out colours of ice creams; they were going to pubs that were once remote, their bars as greasy as the backs of old gas-stoves, but which are now like airport lounges.

After these passages, the silence and stillness closed in again, as the sea closes over the tiny fury of a stone thrown into it.

If two of us met, we'd console each other about the weather, whatever weather it was—if it was sunny, it was too hot, or the brightness hurt one's eyes; if it was cold, it was too cold; if it was wet, it was "always raining". Or we'd take very seriously some petty inconvenience. We'd grumble about the by-laws; or about "them" moving the bus stop fifty yards; or about the public telephone being out of order. This way of grumbling about everything was a sign of being able to contain and accept everything; to say that you "couldn't take anymore" was to show that you could still carry on "taking it".

The calendar of its decay was marked by plagues.

For a year or two, quite inexplicably, many stray, or at least semi-abandoned, dogs menaced the village. One mother, worried about her children's safety, was told by the police that they had no power to rid the village of its dogs until the dogs actually bit someone; but before they bit anyone, the bony, ragged dogs vanished as inexplicably as they came.

At one time the village attracted, through its cheap and easily available housing, families who had proved untrustworthy to pay council-house rents or to take care of their homes. Millbank was the only place in which they could live in the squalor and disorganization that they found comfortable. There were men-less women, who still wanted to look like Marlene Dietrich but who were torn by their children; and women-less men who imagined that they looked like John Wayne. Sometimes they got together; fortunately other people talked quietly about the consequences.

Then there have been plagues of untidiness. One family would begin by stacking old car tyres or an old gas stove or an unwanted chair outside their door—if the Cleansing Department wouldn't move them, if you had neither a car of your own nor the money to hire someone else to take them to the corporation tip, and if you had no land on which to burn or bury them, what else could you do with them? Or one person's dustbin would overflow. Or a dog would regularly visit a dustbin because it had learnt how to tip the lid with its nose and upset the rubbish into the street. Often the plague began with a lapse because of the difficulty of tidying up after children who had only the street in which to play. No sooner had the filth begun to gather in the gutter and to flow around the village, than others would catch-on to the pointlessness of keeping dustbins tidy; and soon, first of all around the dustbins and the lavatories, and eventually the whole village, would smell of neglected drains, urine, and stale food.

Much of the district treated Millbank as a joke; Millbank even joked at itself. The odd one out; the white blackbird; the bald hen that is pecked to death in the hen yard; the scapegoat is necessary to us—we cannot bear ourselves and our weaknesses, apparently, unless we can either feel sorry for, or we can victimize, someone worse off than ourselves. This made things still worse in Millbank. When there are no Joneses to keep up with, people become more squalid.

And when a village is uncertain of its future, it becomes squalid: there is then no point in investing in long-term repairs.

And there was much uncertainty, because the council alternated between apparent apathy and its opposite. There were rumours that the council planned to demolish the village and replace it with a housing estate—naturally, one of those council-house estates that look particularly barren and conspicuous on a Pennine hill-side, though I don't think that the aesthetics worried hardly anyone. They were no more than rumours, fed by the council's policy of putting a closure order on houses as they became empty. Of course, in the situation of the time, no one wanted to give time or money for the "doing up" of these inadequate houses. So they remained empty, and had their windows broken, their fixtures and electric wiring wrecked, their water and gas supplies plundered for the sake of copper and lead piping. With good fortune, some of them were boarded up. Either way, the result was depressingly desolate. No one had money to spend, so the shops gave up, too; and pubs went out of fashion all over England, anyway, during the years after the second world war; so Millbank was without social centres of any kind.

The description I have given is, I think, true to what it was like to live in that fairly typical village house in West Yorkshire during, or shortly before, 1970. People were separated through lack of a social cause. By "cause" I don't necessarily mean the threat of an apocalypse; I mean, also, such causes as the middle-class ones of dinner parties and/or boating clubs; or the working-class ones of band clubs, pub trips, and chapel outings: all of which have been eroded, either from weariness or from confusion caused by social change, in this village at any rate. What social gatherings there were tended to be secretive—like those of the farmers who waited for their privilege of drinking after hours in the pub, impatient for the departure of less-trusted, irregular customers.

Since General Improvement Schemes, my house, like many other houses, has changed; and Millbank like most other West Riding villages (for better or for worse) has altered to become what the new generation of villagers, who are well-heeled, motorized commuters to neighbouring—or not-so neighbouring—towns and cities expect them to be.

Changes to my cottage began in 1972 when I had a bonfire raging for two days and smouldering for a night upon one of the several ruins of Millbank cottages.

I burnt a cellar-full of timber that, after years of propping up the ceilings of other people's houses, being walked upon and swung as other people's floors and doors, had come to retire with me. I had forgotten its various arrivals; and I had tolerated my cellar-clutter because I was sure it would be useful again.

It was. It gave a fine, much needed entertainment to the village kids. Women neighbours, to whom in my two years in this secretive village I hadn't spoken and had hardly met, came out with their rubbish to burn on my fire—so compelling is the chance of a purging; so sociable is fire.

I added broken chairs that I had picked up from a quarry on the moors, and had kept for so long because I promised myself that I'd mend them; three florid lampshades, also from a quarry, where they'd been dumped with other fairground effects (it's amazing what you find in those high, desolate quarries; I once saw a three piece suite arranged around a table in one of them); some porn. that a couple of drunks, to whom I had given a lift one night on the road between Oldham and Halifax, had left in my van, and I had kept, partly because I was too shy to put them in the dustbin (I know a man who works for the Cleansing Department and it's frightening what he's learnt about people from the contents of their dustbins); dull dossiers of letters making arrangements for poetry readings, and some less-dull ones that were better put where they couldn't cause mischief; manuscripts that the mice had chewed and the damp had rotted, so that they weren't worth saving for the day when the University of Texas would be begging for them; and even some fan mail:

Dear Mr Hughes,
    Whilst watching your programme on TV I was startled by the appearance of two spirit figures. Sitting on a stool in your old farmhouse home was an old lady in a big white apron and a cotton sun bonnet. In the junk shop I could plainly see an Indian in a white turban and wearing dark glasses. This is not the first time I have seen these spirits on a TV screen. My friends say I am crackers.

Whilst the fire burned I took van loads of unburnable detritus to the corporation tip; packed my books into boxes (apart from these and a few clothes, I found that I had nothing else worth keeping) and, with my house now empty for the builder, the electrician, the plasterer and the plumber to work in it, I drove to the house of my friend David Pease in Todmorden, where I planned to leave my books, stay for one night, and set off to do something I had never done, but have felt for years that I ought to do: I planned to find out what these borders of Yorkshire and Lancashire, that I knew so well from driving around them, and from one-day walks, would look like and feel like if I walked them for many days on end.

3

DAVID LIVES IN a large, sixteenth-century house called Kilnhurst.

You leave Todmorden by a narrow gully between black terraced houses; cross a black slime that is the River Calder at that point; climb very steeply for about a mile between red-brick semis and bungalows that, after being there for about twenty years, are beginning to look less gauche, amongst their settling lawns and roses and cherry trees (it was spring time, and the gardens were beginning to blossom); and turn a corner that hides the still rather aloof house that gave its name to the road you have climbed and to the vicinity—Kilnhurst.

In West Yorkshire are many such houses, most of them built as opulent homes for those early capitalists, the seventeenth-century wool merchants who gathered the products of others' labour, paid for it, and traded it at a higher price in exchanges like the eighteenth-century Piece Hall in the village of Heptonstall, or in the larger one in Halifax—which trading led them naturally to paying a wage to the people who wove the cloth, in return for all of the work that they did; which led to organizing their work in factories.

The modern world began, in a sense, in such houses; and they are now often neglected because of the unattractiveness of their setting amongst the mills that grew around them; or they are turned into municipal offices, peripheral farms, or restaurants.

At the far side of Kilnhurst, beyond a small level lawn, is the quarry from which came the stone to build the house—though you need to know Pennine quarries quite well in order to recognize it as one, because it must be a few hundred years since it was used, and it is overgrown with stumpy trees and yellow grass, and the hollows between stones have become little marshy places.

It makes a fine background to the house—a grand curve of cliff with the house as its centre. It has the acoustics of an amphitheatre—

you can talk quite quietly near to the top of the cliff, and be heard at the house door.

The setting is also suitably grand for the white horse that stood, becomingly motionless, by one of the quarry's innumerable sun-traps, where the abandoned stones hold off the wind and reflect the sun; and for the man, dressed in a white panama hat, an open-necked shirt, and (as he almost always is) in riding breeches, who lay in the grass by the horse's feet. I thought that the ground must be still damp, and cold, and certainly prickly with clipped rushes and small stones; but the man did not seem to be uncomfortable because of it. He was reading *Paradise Lost*; and he lay between the horse's feet—rather dangerous, you might think, if you did not know the intimate relationship between the man and the horse.

The man is Billy Holt; or William Holt on the covers of his books; or William Holt, publisher on a signboard fixed to the wall of his house. The horse is Trigger. Trigger is, I guess, that man's closest friend. I will guess, also, that no horse ever had such a friend in a man.

Fifteen years ago, Billy Holt saw Trigger pulling a rag and bone cart through Todmorden; and—as Bill describes the moment—the horse seemed unhappily blinkered between the shafts, and he himself was equally blinkered by the walls of the Calder Valley; so it seemed right that man and horse should know each other better. He bought Trigger for five pounds. The man and the horse travelled through France, Italy, Austria, Germany and the Netherlands together—the horse carrying the man, the man caring for the horse, and each keeping the other warm when they slept together in the open—as they still do, sometimes, on the moors above Todmorden.

Earlier in the day, Bill had been to visit an old friend, Ingeborg, in York. Sometimes Ingeborg comes to Todmorden to put his life in order and to clean his house for him. Sometimes—if he wants to enjoy the sun, or to write or to draw something—he objects to her dusting. "The bloody world's made of dust," he says; "we come from dust and we end as dust. Sometimes dust has been very useful to me, when I used to write in it as it fell on the machines in the mill. I'm not going to get upset about a bit of dust when I have more important things to do." This time, Ingeborg had taken him out to eat Chinese spare ribs for the first time in his life.

"I had the pleasure of eating one dish that had a finger bowl with some lemon in it, so you could wipe your fingers afterwards, because this thing you couldn't eat with a fork, not even with chopsticks, you had to take it between your fingers and gnaw it. I had a pleasure like a child, diving into a pie—you know how children get all dirty and enjoy themselves?

"The only place I've seen this is when Mohammedans break the fast of Ramadhan. They really want a meal and they start eating oily rice and mutton with their fingers; in the north we only get that pleasure with fish and chips. How lovely they taste when we eat them in the streets!

"I envy children," he said, "and I envy animals too. In a bar in Todmorden once, where we were getting bored and nothing was comfortable, there was a dog lying on the carpet, so sensual and luxuriant. And I lay down on the carpet with the dog. It was lovely because it was a good carpet, though you can't drink very well lying down.

"We've been so bloody silly. We've lost a lot of the primitive, natural experiences. The irony is that these primitive joys of the caveman are now the privileges of the rich. The rich man goes yachting, and hunting, and his wife wears animal skins, and they both eat meat; what the aristocrat enjoys is what the caveman had. We who are not aristocratic have to put up with nylon shirts and all that modern rubbish. Children—of course they're not so silly, they enjoy themselves and get covered all over in food."

What kind of a life has he had, this man who has the small stature of one who comes from generations of factory workers; this much-travelled man who can take the first experience of eating spare-ribs at the age of nearly seventy-six, and relate it to his knowledge of Mohammedans and to his notion of a proper way to live; who is lying very grandly between the feet of his horse, reading Milton on a working day, in the sun on the moors above a town as active as a furnace; what kind of man is he, this William Holt, author, publisher, traveller, broadcaster, and "veteran member of the Savage Club"; this friend of Dylan Thomas, of Jack Hawkins, of J. B. Priestley, of George Orwell, and of H. G. Wells, who gave him that early—almost, a first—edition of the *Complete Works of Voltaire*, in French that he is quite capable of reading, and which now line two shelves in his part of Trigger's stable?

To question him, I set up a tape recorder on Bill's kitchen table. He was most concerned to address the microphone properly; it was as if he were again broadcasting to America for Lord Reith and the BBC, doing those programmes called *Britain Speaks* which, according to him, helped to bring America to our side during the second world war. Unnecessarily careful because of his age, I begged him to sit down, but he insisted on standing before the microphone; he was concerned because I might pick up background sounds. His thought related himself to the whole history of man; and more particularly, to the Industrial Revolution, here in Yorkshire.

"I was an offspring of the pioneers of the Industrial Revolution, the weavers and the spinners who took the blitz of the machines, that came out of space to them, on the chin; and now they lie under the sod. They haunt me, the spirits of those men and women and even children who had to take this terrible invasion of the machinery into their lives. Those weavers and spinners haunt me, the mill-wrights and engineers and early pioneers of the Industrial Revolution who carried on almost ignored by the rest of the world who were too concerned with Dionysus and the Napoleonic Wars and all kinds of things that were happening south of this region.

"Right before the pyramids of Egypt, all through human history two hands had spun one thread with the spinning wheel. This extends to the time of George Washington. Then there came a man, almost illiterate, a weaver, who spun eight threads and then spun ten threads and then eighty threads and then 120 threads, with only two hands—one hand turning the wheel and the other hand drawing out the cotton. That was James Hargraves; and until recently there wasn't even a plaque, let alone a monument recording his name; but a few years ago a fuss was made by a few people like me and a small garden of remembrance has been made near where he was born just above Oswaldtwistle. As the crow flies it's only about ten miles from where we're sitting now in this barn so we're practically within the walls of the cradle of the Industrial Revolution. Because these extra threads were spun by turning a handle on this machine made of bits of wood and brass it was possible to speed up production and this led to water frames and steam engines. And even now, in this region, there's this curious engineering character of the old millwrights, who applied science to practical life. Sir John Cockcroft, who helped split the atom, and really found the philosopher's stone, turning baser metals into gold, was born in Todmorden. Two Nobel prizewinners were born in this little town of Todmorden—Sir John Cockcroft, and a fellow called Wilkinson, a chemist. Isn't that amazing?—and there isn't a memorial to either of them. Cockcroft, before he split the atom, when he lived round here as a boy, built an electric system into their mill, John Cockcroft and Sons at Walsden. I knew him very well and he was sorry its spin off was the atom bomb.

"Right from my earliest days my thoughts were rebellious against authority. The first authority was my family; before I could even talk I ran away several times. Once my mother tied me to the railings outside our little terraced house in Joshua Street and one of my aunts who was sorry for me released me.

"The authority of the school came next, because it was boring. My parents sent me to school very early to get what they called discipline. Discipline was to stop you being what you really are, that is it was the opposite of education—instead of drawing out of you what you are, they tried to make you into something else.

They sent me when I was three, and I wouldn't have it. There was an attempt to discipline me by using the cane; this inspired my first work of art, a mural decoration. When they put me to bed I got out my materials and drew the teacher with a cane in her hand and extended the cane all the way round the four walls of the bedroom to the back of the teacher where there was a small boy receiving the cane. That was my first work of art, inspired by rebellion. I was about three.

"I revolted against theology in the Sunday Schools. I was deeply religious in that I was fascinated by the mystery of existence: Who was I? Why was I here? What was it all about? I wasn't satisfied by the explanation given by my Sunday School teacher, who was a Nonconformist Wesleyan. I objected to all the stuff that was wrapped around Jesus. It was quite simple to understand what he said, it all seemed quite reasonable to me, but there was such a lot of talk about the others in the Bible, especially St Paul. He was quite a person was St Paul, writing letters to explain all sorts of things. I said, 'Yes, I know. I take it for granted. Why bother about all that? Let's get back to Jesus.' Because I kept getting back to Jesus' 'Sermon On The Mount' and so on my Uncle Will, who was a Sunday School teacher, said I was drifting towards Unitarianism— Unitarianism looks upon Jesus as a human person and doesn't bother much about his supernatural origins. But I'm not a Unitarian. I'm what you might call a Nonconformist who doesn't conform with the Nonconformists—that's a funny sort of rebellion, isn't it?

"What I do remember is the old second-hand bookseller who was the principal teacher of the young men's class. He was a very sincere fellow and he gave this extraordinary apology for St Paul. He said, 'Thou art after a bare-legged religion, art tha?' He said, 'Thou wouldn't go down the street without thee breeches on, wouldst tha?' 'No,' I said. 'Then let thee dress thee religion up,' he said. 'The glory of Jesus will shine through all the wrappings that either thee or St Paul can put around him.'

"And right enough, the glory of Jesus does shine through every attempt to decorate him or veil him or transfigure him. Even John

Wesley, for instance. Though he was a Conservative and a re-
actionary he couldn't hide the teaching of Jesus.

"When I was twelve I began half-time at the mill. One week
I had to work mornings starting at six o'clock; and then on alternate
weeks I worked afternoons. Like the other half-timers, I felt sleepy
when I went to school in the afternoon. The teachers put all the
half-timers on the back row and if we fell asleep they didn't wake
us. So I didn't learn much at school. I went full-time to the mill
when I was thirteen and then I had to work fifty-six hours a week—
ten hours a day, and Saturday mornings.

"The noise of the machinery of weaving is a monotonous roar
so loud that you can't hear your own voice even if you shout;
people communicate by lip-reading like deaf-and-dumb people.
This noise became like a silence to me: nobody could interrupt me.
I could think for hours and hours at a time; I was out in the wilder-
ness, alone like the Old Testament prophets. I began to learn
languages, for their sheer beauty—I didn't care about examinations
and I'd no plans but I wanted to read the classics in the original
and the great writers in all the different languages. I started with
German, because the Gothic letters were so beautiful. I was able to
recite German in the roar of the looms without anyone skitting
me: they couldn't hear what I was saying and they couldn't lip-
read either, because it was German. There's a constant falling of dust
from cotton weaving. It's part of the size and the china clay. Like
you can write on a mirror when you breathe on it, you can write in
the dust that falls on the steel machines, then rub it off and soon the
dust settles again. I wrote my first exercise in German in that dust.

"After the discipline of school, and the mill, there was the discipline of the army, in 1914. I didn't much mind that, there was
action and we were fighting for some purpose. The army released
me from this valley and gave me an opportunity to use my talents.
One thing it insisted upon was: never let the enemy take the
initiative, you take it and you'll always be right. In writing home to
my mother and father I began to be interested in what was coming
into my own letters when I described a cabbage field in the rain

looking like scales. I thought it was nice to think of things like that so I developed letter-writing in the army.

"I dived into politics in that period when the winds of change were blowing pretty violently. I met a lot of prominent politicians, Harry Pollitt and so on; many of them visited my home and all I could give them was bread and butter, and not even that sometimes. My joining the Communist Party was speeded up by the debate that took place in Parliament on Socialism. They said that Socialism wouldn't work because human nature wasn't good enough. There's a certain amount of truth in it—I know that human nature is bewildered, ignorant, and has been very unkindly treated. But I have great faith in human nature in its deepest state: it is capable of greatness.

"I joined the Communist Party, not because of wages or rent or taxation, but as a rebel in defence of human nature. I was a bit of a quixotic fellow and I began to tilt at the bloody windmills, like Sir Alfred Mond. I was given nine months' imprisonment for protesting against the harsh administration of the Means Test. I consider my imprisonment to have been a privilege. I fought an election campaign for the town council from my prison cell and failed by only a handful of votes to unseat the ex-deputy mayor, who was one of the magistrates who sent me to prison. When I came out I got a terrific majority in Stansfield ward which was the old Conservative ward that had never been taken by either Liberals or Labour and I got it as an out-and-out left-winger; I won three elections in a row, though they tried to unseat me by putting three up and splitting the vote and all that. I went abroad as a correspondent for Kemsley Newspapers and because I couldn't attend committee meetings I resigned. There was a clash with the Communist Party, who objected to my resigning without consulting them.

"I called myself a member of the Communist Party of Great Britain; but I wasn't really an orthodox Communist. It nauseated me to do my first task as a Communist, which was to cause unrest in mills for demands for better lavatories—which of course you need, but it was urgent to think on a far grander scale than that. But the Communists said you had to get the people moving on issues they are willing to fight for; as they fight for these small issues, and meet opposition, they see where that opposition is coming from and they learn the class war. It's sound as far as it goes, but my interests have been much wider. Because I was more interested in the aesthetic side of life, I sent a letter to the *Daily Worker* in which I said I wanted to get in touch with other men and women who are interested in founding a league for the liberation of proletarian art, writing and painting and poetry expressed through personal vision, which they were not able to do under the capitalist system of the day. They wouldn't publish it, and said it was against the rules of the Communist Party to found a united front on any issue without it coming from the top. I said, 'All right, do it from the top'. 'No,' they said, 'It's useless. You can't revolutionize proletarian art until you've had the revolution. You've to wait for that.' And I disagreed. I said that all this was part of the movement; there were some like myself who would fight to the death defending art and the right to express personal vision. I felt about the Communists—as I felt about the scientists—that their ends were my beginnings. I'm with them in the search for their ends but I'm interested in what comes beyond that—the inner, the real mystery, the inner mystery of it all.

"I've travelled in about forty-three countries by now. I was guest of Mr Nehru and we had a heart to heart talk; and Dr Radha-krishnan before he was president invited me to dinner and I had a talk to him about East and West and that sort of thing. Not so much a political talk but more on mystical problems. I've lived with a holy man in India in his cave and discussed his views of these questions of existence. I went to the Spanish Civil War as a war correspondent for Kemsley Newspapers. I also travelled in Russia, where, though I didn't actually meet Stalin, I met a lot of the other Kremlin people.

"I went to Russia just after the Revolution. After arriving by sea at Leningrad we were put into a very large luxury hotel that had been converted into a hostel: there were camp beds all over the place, as many beds as they could get into one room. I'd only been in the place for a few hours when I heard a noise in the street. Coming from England, that was in a state of almost riotous assembly through three million unemployed, and the Means Test, my first impression was that there was a demonstration against the government—any noise or singing in the street, to me, meant a demonstration; and all our demonstrations had been anti-State. I looked out of the window and I saw a lot of people, many of them young, standing at a stopping place for a tramcar. They were singing at the tops of their voices and they looked happy. I said to the interpreters, 'Who are these people?' They said, 'They are the Sobotniki. These are the men and women who have done their week's work and are now on holiday and are going to help the farmers without pay.'"

Bill put his hand to his face; he was crying.

"I can't remember them and talk about it without deep emotion. These Sobotniki were what I wanted to be and what I believed was the very heart of political Communism and they were singing and they were happy and they made me happy. But where are the Sobotniki now? That was forty years ago."

Bill paused for quite a long while. There was nothing I wanted to say.

"What I despise most is meanness. My reaction to anything that's mean is to do the very opposite. I was once selling bags of coal in Todmorden when I was hard up. I hadn't any capital, and I used to order on credit a waggon load of coal at the railway. If I could get six or seven orders I hired a horse and a man and a cart to deliver the coal. A woman on the street there ordered two bags of coal. I lifted the grating on the street and shot the coal down the chute and the lying swine came out and said she didn't order those bags—but she'd taken good care to see they'd gone down the chute before she said she didn't order them. My reaction—it was a bit Don Quixotic really—was to put another bag down. It was bloody silly, but I gave her another bag.

"It's rather odd that I, born as a working man, should have a great admiration for true aristocratic life. At the microphone I had a long argument with C. M. Joad; he rather lost his temper with me in one of two broadcasts under the title 'The Meaning Behind The Word'. The word that we were discussing was 'aristocracy'. He argued that aristocracy no longer meant what it used to mean. He said that it now means a man who was either born in a certain bed or who lined his pockets more successfully or who was clever at politics.

"I said, 'That's not aristocracy. Even if he's been born in a certain bed if that's the way they live they cease to be aristocrats. They are declassed. Among the true aristocrats they would be kicked out—bounders, you know.'

"I insisted that there is in the world and in life room for aristocracy and that I admire the aristocrat. There are some who are born natural aristocrats. I still feel that the true aristocrat can be recognized at once in the man's attitude to life and it has nothing to do with money. I have met a few and I've noticed this: that the common people recognize it when they're personally present. When the aristocrat gets up to go out the common people open doors for him; his manners are such that they inspire from the people a response, and that is aristocracy. And there isn't a great difference between the proper craftsman and the aristocrat, you know; though socially they're wide apart. We have produced in this region proud craftsmen in all the crafts—very proud and not corrupt, generous and believers in truth and decent behaviour.

"My main art in life has been life itself. I was not dissatisfied. What I've had and what I have is good. I love it. Every bit of it. Every minute of it. So I'm not dissatisfied. But I'm unsatisfied; unsatisfied means you like what's on the menu but there isn't enough of it.

"I've had to work for my living all my life; and when I went to see the head of the Third Programme once and I'd had terrific success broadcasting to America during the war and all over the place I said, 'Aren't you interested in the outlook of a working

man in the present world situation and who is articulate and has
written books?' He said: 'But you're not a working man'; and I
thought, 'Well, that's a bugger! I've been working all my damned
life!' All this Evelyn Waugh snobbery and that set-up—well, to
Hell with the damned lot of them."

4

THE NEXT MORNING, when I planned to set off on my walk, there was an out-of-season snow storm. It obliterated the landscape so violently, you wouldn't turn a dog out to it. Whirlpools of snow filled the air, in the place of a firm and familiar landscape of stones in the crevices of which the wiry grass was beginning to turn into a trickle of green; in place of a landscape of dark factories and trees thickening with emerging leaves. I stayed in bed; regretted it in the afternoon when the storm quietened; and spent the afternoon hours shopping in Todmorden for food for an evening meal.

Todmorden is at the convergence of two valleys. It is therefore approached by three roads, each road lined with terraced houses and with shops, many of which are empty. These roads lead to the usual kind of town centre, with uncomfortable cafés; Hellenic public buildings; and the shops of monopolies that have robbed the smaller shops of trade. Despite a local feeling that the livelihoods of local people need supporting, here, as in all the small towns, the chain stores for groceries, for electric goods, for furniture, have been encouraged to establish themselves, thus aiding the movement of money out of the town; and thus helping to establish an alien and impersonal architecture right at the town centre, where it brings about the rotting of the community life outside that centre.

But Todmorden shops seem, by the very nature of their trade, to be doomed anyway. For how much longer will people want the clog-maker—on the Burnley Road, just beyond the market—with his tiny window dripping with leather straps, and with boots and shoes and clogs hanging by their laces? I went into a tobacconist's —and I *mean* a tobacconist's, who sold pipes and tobacco that was kept in mahogany drawers; who had framed 1920s adverts on the walls; and a cane chair with a painted advert half-ground off its backrest by the backs that had rested against it, in the days when you needed a rest whilst you waited your turn in the tobacconist's. The tobacconist had time to talk. He told me he hadn't much stock left because he was quitting the business. Apparently no one wanted to take the business over; he said the reason was that a tobacconist's shop was too expensive to stock.

All three roads focus on the most immediately impressive building in Todmorden: the Town Hall. It seems disproportionately large for its town; and being one of the few buildings to be cleaned, its whiteness makes it more conspicuous. Like most Victorian architecture, its proportions are absurdly at variance with the monumental intentions expressed in its size and in its details; so that rather than impressing in a monumental way, it instead scales everything, including itself, down. It has the scale of a Victorian clock dominating a mantelpiece. Around it, dividing its classical columns, are unfilled niches designed for statues—maybe they should put a statue of Bill Holt in one of them, and of Trigger in another, someday.

On these buildings is the mark of confidence; of certainty; of an unmistakable belief that they were making something new and great. It is the mark of all nineteenth-century buildings in every city, town and village in the industrial north. The poet Norman Nicholson calls these places "The Athens of the Industrial Revolution". They have the confidence that a new thing believed-in inspires. Their heavy-handed confidence was to transform most of the world; and these buildings seem to remind me that they almost realized that it would happen. All buildings, and not just churches, are "sermons in stone"—of a kind. I think of West Yorkshire building as being thoroughly done in a most soulless, humourless way; they are monuments to work, and to what can be achieved by work. What can be achieved by work alone is demonstrated for future generations when they look to the tops of high walls built by their ancestors certain that they were founding dynasties with chapels, swimming baths, prisons, town halls, and see huge stones, unnecessarily large, that have been heaved to immense heights by Heaven-knows what strength, or ingenuity with pulleys or other

machines of which West Yorkshire is traditionally proud that it
invented or made: the 367 feet high chimney that was built in
sixteen weeks at Blinkhorn's chemical works, Bolton, in 1842 ("a
circumstance unparalleled in the history of the world", crowed the
Bolton Chronicle), and up which 4,000 people were hauled, four
at a time in a basket, to admire the view from the top before the
chimney was used; or the 435-feet-high chimney built in 1846 at
Wallgate, Wigan, but which collapsed into the canal, so that a man
on the canal bank who fell into the canal was driven to the other
side of it by waves created by the falling stone—comical buildings
without a sense of humour, and monuments to work.

It was lunch time (only it's called "dinner time") and the shops were
shut. I didn't much mind. I went into a dark pub that smelled of
urine and stale beer from the night before. An unlit juke-box made
it seem particularly inhospitable. There was one customer, who
took half an hour to tell me the three-minutes-long story about
the Todmorden lady who, because she was told that her postal
address was in Lancashire, went to the post office to find out where
she really lived, and when told that she did live in Yorkshire replied,
"Thank God for that! They say they have terrible weather in
Lancashire." As everyone knows, if only from cricket, the distinction
between Yorkshire and Lancashire is a most important one: the
drawing of the differences goes back to the Wars of the Roses.
Most people who particularly like one of these counties have an
equal dislike for the other; usually, they prefer the county in which
they were born. Frequently Lancashire people find Yorkshire
people unfriendly; or Yorkshire people find Lancashire people so.
"Yorkshire is all hills and moors; Lancashire is all mills and whores"
is one definition of the differences between the counties. People
claim to be able to tell where the boundary is by an unmistakable
change of atmosphere that strangers are unable to distinguish. I
know a Yorkshire lady who claims she can tell that she has passed
into Lancashire when "well-made, well-kept stone houses give way

to mean, brick streets"; I know a Lancashire man who says he recognizes passage into Yorkshire by the black pompous building. Some difference of this kind undoubtedly does exist; though what words you choose to describe it depends, of course, on your attitude.

To get the man off his subject, I asked him if he knew William Holt.

"Billie 'Olt!" he exclaimed. Then he added sarcastically, "Willie 'Olt of Todmorden, I don't reckon nowt to him."

But before he would say any more, he asked me if I knew him.

"I know him a little. What's wrong with him?" I asked.

"*Trigger Through Europe* and all that? That's all right; but it's what he wrote about people here that I don't like. What he wrote about his wife. He's done what he wanted to, has Willie Holt," he said reproachfully; "Good luck to him," he added, as if he meant the opposite.

The prejudice against someone who goes his own way, and proves that he doesn't need any special advantage to do it! For this man, Willie Holt's gesture of escape was like a slap in the face.

I left the pub early, and having nothing better to do I looked for a greengrocer's shop that might be open during the dinner hour. I found one which, though its door was unlocked, was unlit; beyond the shop, in the living quarters, a man and a woman were eating dinner. I felt like an intruder. Then the woman mumbled "coming" with her mouth full of food. On each of their plates, a tiny piece of meat amongst a mass of over-boiled potatoes and cabbage floated on gravy coloured with "browning": the food that is responsible for the idea that English cooking is the worst in the world. On the linoleum, a hairy black cat gnawed selfishly at what seemed to me to be quite a good steak; the cat saw me, and perhaps thought I was going to steal its meat, for it slunk off with it. The woman stood up and squealed at the cat in baby-talk: "Come on, Nigger! Nigger! Nigger! Nigger!" Because the cat took no notice, she tried saying more softly: "Come on, then." The cat scowled far off, though she coaxed it. The man got off his chair and stooped to the cat, perhaps to suggest to the woman that she should serve me in the shop. She served me without looking at me. I looked at her: she had the mournful face of someone used to tearful occasions. Then I asked her for green peppers; this made her curious, and she looked at me. Her face seemed ten years younger. "Don't mind me asking, luv," she said, "but what do you do with them?"

I spent the evening drinking and smoking too much; packed a rucksack with inadequate clothes; and set off at six o'clock the next morning. The earth was rigid with a scattering of frozen snow and little was distinguishable in the grey light; but larks were singing at a height from which they could see the sun rising beyond the hills. The sky was absolutely clear; the stars faded into it as it became blue slowly. The noises of Todmorden and the Calder Valley were the more insistent because of this dawn quiet.

I skirted the broken hillside above Lumbutts; where gulls were screaming over the tip I turned to follow the stream through the thin oak woods and the scatterings of farms, intending to follow the paved pack-horse road that climbs the moor to that gross monument to the Battle of Waterloo, Stoodley Pike. Though I could not yet see it, the sun had now risen high enough to touch the lip of the valley above me. The sunshine was like a light thrust into a coal cellar, making the snow on the rocks glitter like eyes, and seeming to further darken this valley.

I climbed on to the rim of a plateau; as I crossed the plateau the noises of the Calder Valley were suddenly shut off. A different world! The plateau carried a maze of tiny, stone-walled, well-kept fields to the foot of the moor. Peewits rose and tumbled in the air.

I skirted the farm where, from a distance, I had roused the dogs to barking. These dogs set the dogs at the next farm to barking, and those dogs stirred others; so I felt that I had aroused and alarmed the peaceful, pastoral world, even though no one and nothing but one farm dog and a few birds had seen me.

It was a long time since I'd been about the world so early in the morning. I'd imagined that I'd be the only person awake. But when, following the walls, I stumbled into their centre—a tiny hamlet, a farm and some cottages near Mankinholes—it was as busy as at any time during the day. I could hear a milking machine; a man who crossed the yard with a bucket disregarded me, as if it were the most usual thing for someone to be walking past at this time— and I feeling so adventurous, and frightened of waking people!— and a woman was cleaning the insides of her windows.

The woman and I met eye to eye. It seemed insulting to carry on walking. I hesitated. She put her wash-leather down carefully amongst plastic flowers and shining ornaments and she came to the door. She confronted me with an expectant smile, as if I were an expected bearer of good news—maybe it was just because it was morning; the hens in the yard, with their combs shining red in the light, seemed so relaxed. I pretended that I didn't know my way. She directed me around the verge of a mill pool, which had attractively broken down so that it looked like a natural pond, with reeds and with ducks pecking amongst them, to the path that, even at this distance—I was about a mile from it—seemed so stark as it climbed to Stoodley Pike.

I went back to Mankinholes. There I entered one of those characteristically gloomy Pennine lanes, that seem so unnecessarily high-walled. The high black walls shut out most of the light, so that only the wiriest grass grew on the banks; the surface was brutally stony.

The roadway soon led to a gate to the open moor. The bog is crossed by a line of paving stones that reach, like a ladder to Heaven, straight up the moor to Stoodley Pike. This is the old pack-horse road, leading to Lancashire. The pavement has been worn into a trough. Each stone is saddle-shaped, worn that way by the feet that have trodden it—like the stones of mill stairs and church steps and the staired footpaths in the villages. In the trough worn in the stones I could see bubbles of air running downhill under the ice. Near to the top, without apparent cause, the pavement turns in a right angle, and after a few yards turns as geometrically to the left again; because there seems to be nothing to circumvent, the path seems very odd here.

Seeing which way the path went, and seeing no reason for it, I decided to cut the corner and climb directly through the rushes to Stoodley Pike. Some mounds of stone, presumably left over from quarrying to build the monument, cut off sight of the Pike, and also of the pavement; extraordinarily quickly, I found myself lost in a vast scoop of moor. I cut back, and came on to the monument from the rear, as it were—which was fortunate, for then I found, in surprise, the panorama of the valley out of which I had climbed.

I am told that one's eye automatically enlarges something seen on the skyline; but to see Stoodley Pike only from the valley, as a mark on the crest of the hill, is to have no idea of the remarkable size of this obelisk—not that it isn't typical of such monuments. Like all the others, Stoodley Pike is black and lugubrious and faintly Egyptian. Rather than being celebratory or joyous, it is funereal—which is perhaps as proper an attitude to the war that it marks, as any other attitude. Architecturally, the main thing that it achieves is to disappointingly reduce the scale of its surrounding hills.

On each of its four sides there are arched recesses. The one that faced the sun also, fortunately, cut out the slight but icy wind, and I sat in it to rest and to look at my map for a way into Hebden Bridge; but I'm a bad map reader, in spite of Mr Murdoch. Because I could see no obvious route, I set off in the direction that I thought Hebden Bridge must be in. On the way downhill, I found a tiny flowering rush, yellow with pollen in the snow.

5

I SUPPOSE THAT the first people to give this region a consciousness were the Brontë sisters; Haworth, with which they are associated, is about ten miles from Hebden Bridge. Consistent with the obtuseness of characters in Brontë novels, to pronounce the word "Haworth" correctly, you must perversely reverse the position of its vowels, and say "Howarth".

The Brontë sisters were here because their father, Patrick, came from Ireland to become the vicar of Haworth. Haworth was a difficult patch for him to work; one of his predecessors had been driven from the church, in mid-service, by his congregation. But Patrick Brontë had a strong personality. He immured, as well as he could, his family in the Parsonage, where they died off, one by one, before him—his wife; all five of his daughters; and his son (who died of drug addiction).

The son, Branwell; and the daughters Charlotte, Emily and Anne; gave most of their lives to the articulation and depicting of unanalysed fantasies, by means of poems, novels, letters, water colours and oil paintings. The place was (and still would be) apt to their obsessions; the energy of its weather, the mystery of its spaces, the distances from the stranger of its self-absorbed people, is a mirror in which a range of fantasies might be discovered. The Brontës must have seemed as incongruous in Haworth during the nineteenth century as does, for instance, Sylvia Plath, the equally unlikely, equally obsessive, American poet, in the nearby and very similar village of Heptonstall, where she lived and is buried. (In fact, if you really want an idea of what Haworth was like when the Brontës were alive, you would do much better to visit Heptonstall— at the moment, anyhow. For Heptonstall seems about to turn into another Haworth.)

Once you know what kind of life is really lived beneath the

surface of Haworth's glittering tourism, you realize that the Brontës, and what they represent, are as incongruous as they ever were.

But that's the under-life. On the surface, no guilt at having spurned the Brontës, a little, as "queer folk" whilst they lived troubles Haworth now. On any fine weekend the street through Haworth—kept narrow by a fortunate reluctance to widen it at the expense of houses crowded on both sides, and kept cobbled by the diligence of Brontë romantics—is as noisy and crowded with cars, coaches, and pedestrians, as Oxford Street is at Christmas. One or two policemen wrestle with traffic that is almost immobile; and pedestrians without a pavement squeeze against the house walls, in the blue smoke of exhaust fumes.

Two things bring these predominantly old, or young, people here. Mostly they now come for the Railway Museum in Oakworth, at the bottom of Haworth Hill, on the old railway station and the line where the film *The Railway Children* was made; but, of course, there is still the romantic pull of the Brontës. The custodian of the Brontë Museum says that Haworth is "second only to Stratford for numbers of visitors". I asked him why he thought people were so interested in the Brontës and he answered, "They wrote good, clean, imaginative love stories."

The museum for which he cares is a mirror of the interest that the Brontës inspire. Its cases contain the minutiae of a nineteenth-century spinster's life: a bonnet and a wreath that might (or might not) have held Charlotte's veil in place upon it; Charlotte's mittens, boots, and work basket; the hat "said to have been worn by Ellen Nussey at Charlotte's wedding"; Anne's "small box"; a pincushion said to have belonged to Ellen Nussey; a smelling salts bottle; a nail brush; a cap and collar "said to have been worn by Aunt Branwell"; and "THE ACTUAL TRUNK" (it says in big letters) that Charlotte bought in Brussels. I suppose that for most people who visit these fetishes, the Brontës represent the best of "romantic novelists", believing romantic to mean unlikely, but passionate and non-utilitarian love-affairs—like King Cophetua and the beggar maid; or Heathcliffe and Cathy. They see the Brontës as the beginning of the tradition of Georgette Heyer and Phyllis Bentley. The museum custodian also claims that the beauty of the surrounding countryside attracts the visitors; and I suspect that their modern pilgrims share with the Brontë sisters a romantic attitude to nature, and particularly to the energetic weather of the Haworth moors, as the object of orgiastic fantasies. Haworth, I think, might have faded into the lost atmosphere of holiday places of the past—like Scarborough, for instance—were it not for the Railway Museum. The miraculous revival (in fact, trebling) of local trade, just when it might have been expected to fade out, in consequence of a film company choosing Haworth as a place to shoot a film, seems to justify what one shop owner described as "the spirit of buoyant hope" that typifies Haworth traders, who, though most of them have other jobs outside their shops, have a persistent belief that they will become rich because of wealthy American visitors. Maybe all this is just as well—Haworth, after all, might have literally collapsed into the ground, had it not been for the Brontë trade.

As they approach Haworth, from Keighley or from the Hebden Bridge road, most of these visitors must at first, I fancy, be disappointed. Beyond an untidy straggle of mills, they must approach through a quite usual, messy housing estate, with only the first of those supposedly magic signs, "Brontë Tours", to excite them. So far as I know, *The Railway Children* haven't spawned any trade marks yet; but Brontë insignia mark out the village and some of its surroundings. There are, of course, Brontë Cafés; there are also two shops called Brontë Books (one is the post office); a Brontë Street; a Brontë Tweedmill; and there's a place just outside Haworth where you can buy a warmed-up hamburger, and is called a Brontë sandwich.

Haworth village, preserved as it is, bears about the same resemblance to the actuality of the Brontës' Haworth as does, say, a Christmas card to the reality of Georgian life—it's a sentimentalized lie. Its life is split decisively in two: there is the tourist's Haworth; and there is the rather closely guarded, secretive undercurrent of life typical of all Yorkshire villages—excepting that here it is particu-

Northerners on holiday

Northerners

Moorland Road

Wesley Place, Sowerby

Millbank

Billy Holt and Trigger

Workers talking in a mill

The Calder Valley

Clog-maker's near Keighley

Path to the "Brontë Waterfall"

In Haworth

Heptonstall

Street in the Calder Valley

Todmorden Town Hall

Heptonstall again

Hardibutts Farm, used as an early Methodist meeting place

Crimsworth Dean Chapel, built to replace Hardibutts Farm

Birchcliffe Baptist Chapel, Hebden Bridge

Adelaide Shaw (*extreme right*) in 1913

Mill girls at Leigh Mills, Pudsey

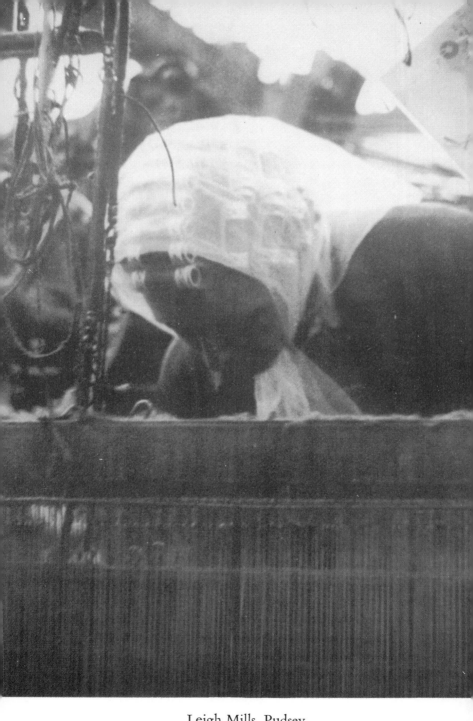

Leigh Mills, Pudsey

Wainhouse Tower, Halifax

Demolition

Wycoller Hall (or Ferndean Manor in *Jane Eyre*)

Staley Hall

Light on the moors

The Tame Valley

Saddleworth Moors

Mossley

The Tame Valley

Haymaking at Intake Farm

Milking

A corner of the farm

larly resistant to the outsider. It could almost be said that Haworth
life is polarized around two pubs; there is The Bull at the top of the
hill, which is for the tourists; and there is The Fleece near the
bottom, whose dingy front intimidates strangers.

In the dark of the Fleece, where there is a juke-box and where
the beer and the sandwiches are very good, and the only signs of
Haworth's associations are photographs of the cast of *The Railway
Children* (who used to drink there: I've noticed before how film
crews and actors have an instinct for the best pubs), I heard a story
about Haworth's brass band. At some date in the past, the band
won an all-England competition at the Crystal Palace. Returning
home late and merry, the band leader told his bandsmen that having
enjoyed a jolly holiday was no reason for waking the whole village;
so the bandsmen took their shoes off to walk up the village street—
still playing their instruments. (I told this story in another place,
and found that it was also told of their local band, so where the
origin of the story is I don't know; not that it matters.)

At the end of the street beyond tourist Haworth is a much neater,
smaller, bit of housing development, maybe intended to make up
for the messiness at the bottom of the hill. Haworth tried hard
enough with it to win a Civic Trust Award—it says so, on a conspicuous plaque. (It's also the only example of architectural punning
I've ever seen: it's called Heath Cliff. But maybe the pun's uninten-
tional.)

Excepting on a weekday, when Haworth has a normal life, I'm afraid
I'm always glad to get away from it.

The footpaths on to the moors are easy to find. Follow the only
road, past Heath Cliff, the public lavatories and a few vicarage-like
houses, and a deserted quarry, and at the point where, deterred by
the useless blankness of untraversable moors, it turns back on itself
and returns on a loop to Keighley, there begins a wide, well-trodden
footpath that was part of Emily's daily walk, and is now sign-
posted "The Brontë Waterfalls".

E

It begins with, usually, parked cars, whose optimistic occupants have set off walking. Except in unusually dry weather, the path is very muddy, like a gateway through which a herd of cattle regularly tread. It travels along the side of the hill interestingly called Enshaw Knoll—presumably before, not after Catherine Earnshaw. Below is Lower Laithe Reservoir, which is the reason for a scattering of beautiful little farmhouses along this track being empty—the Water Boards like to buy up all the property within the catchment areas of reservoirs (which means most of the Pennine moors, I'm afraid) to prevent humans, who might pollute the water with excrement, from living in them. It really amounts to the same activity as the Highland clearances in Scotland and Ireland during the last few centuries. Beyond the reservoir is the village of Stanbury, with its lovely, soft grey outline sliding off as gracefully as a line of music along the slope of its bare hill.

The footpath travels through boulders and dips to the little fall of water called The Brontë Waterfall. Beyond it the path is less well-trodden; not many people reach any more of the "places of interest" on the map in the museum. The waterfall is the last spur to fantasies about the Brontës until you've made the steep climb to the huddle of stones speculatively called Wuthering Heights. The few true Brontë romantics you might meet up here are likely to be flushed with heart palpitations and adventure-excitement; and as much interested in stopping to rest their feet, recover their normal heart-beat, or have a pee behind the stones, as in looking over the building. There is very little to see, anyway. They might be awestruck by its site—it is most dramatic, one way or another, in most kinds of weather—but it is no more than one rectangle of partly-fallen walls without a roof, and a lean-to recently roofed with zinc. Though it could never have even slightly resembled the rather grand house described by Emily Brontë as Wuthering Heights, Top Withens, as it is actually called, is the only building, or ruin of a building, on many miles of moorland, so there is nothing else to compete with it.

Recently some secondary-school children have had a go at

restoring Withens. You can see some wasteful cementing—which is surprising, really, when you think of the effort of getting cement to this place. But the Water Board, who own Top Withens, made them stop. They wouldn't take the risk of someone being injured, for which they weren't insured.

From Top Withens is a footpath over Withens Height and Wadsworth Moor. This is a regular hikers' route and is part of the Pennine Way. Anyone you meet here, outside barbarous grouse-shooting holidays, is likely to be well-shod, wear para-military clothes, carry half-a-hundred-weight of rucksack with varying cheerfulness and greet you with the bonhomie proper to explorers.

Beside the path near to the crown of Wadsworth Moor is a tiny cairn of stones dedicated to the memory of a hiker. It says, "E. Wilkinson. A Rambler. Died August 31 1964 aged 75." Not that he died there. Rather than being a warning that you might expire on this difficult country, it is the expression of a sentiment: one man loved it so much, it is here he wished to be remembered.

Across the moors you can see, conspicuously white, the Pack Horse pub; on 12 August there are so many cars and people huddled around it, so many gun shots, you would think it was besieged.

The path reaches downwards to the lugubrious Walshaw Dean reservoirs. Despite its great open space, this is, to me, a horribly marked landscape, broken by grouse-shooting butts, the unnaturally rigid outlines of the sheets of water, the incongruous rhododendron bushes, and the ecclesiastical-looking waterman's house.

The stream that runs out of Walshaw Dean soon begins to gather spindly trees along its banks; these eventually gather into a spur of the woodlands that people call Hardcastle Crags—the crags being a huddle of stones in the lip of the valley.

The spring sunlight and warmth revitalized me and, it seemed, every other animal and plant. I felt an upsurge of life in the birds that shone in the lit air; in the plants that seemed to be uncurling about me—if I couldn't actually see them uncurling, it seemed to me that I could smell them; it was as if the plants gave off a heavy sweat from the energy used in their uncurling. Shadows flickered in a ceremonious dance over the flank of the moor; from time to time the light swept through the wood on an edge of cold.

Suddenly, I heard a squealing of animals, down by the stream, and hidden from me by the bank. I crept to the top of the bank to see what it was. Amongst the stones of the stream, two stoats copulated and played with one another. They rolled together and nipped one another, only a few feet from me, on the other bank; then one freed itself, and ran under an overhanging root, and re-appeared a few feet off.

The one left behind looked at me, pausing a few moments to do so. Stoats are the shyest of creatures and I was only eight feet from him. (I suppose it was "him", this one being the chaser.) He stared at me coolly for a few moments; then decided, evidently, that I didn't matter today.

He ran after his mate and chased her back to near where I was— as if he were showing her off to me. On this return, the two stoats flushed a rabbit out of the bank. A rabbit, that is usually terrified of a stoat; that is usually transfixed by its terror! But this rabbit, realizing that it wasn't to be hunted at this moment, hopped a few feet from the track of the stoats, and squatted, licking its paws. The rabbit wasn't afraid of me, either. If it wasn't scared of a stoat, why should it be frightened of me?

After another shameless roll, the stoats ran together. (By together, I mean literally together, like one ball rolling itself, hardly stirring a leaf, and with no noise from its movement, only from its squeals.)

Then they returned.

Taking courage from the rabbit I sat on the top of the bank, without trying to be secretive, and I watched.

All along the stream through the woods that day, the water-ouzels were singing from the stones; and every creature seemed pre-occupied with itself, or with its mate. It seemed a day when no creature hunted, or hurt another; as if the sexual energy about me had brought an immense peacefulness with it.

The woods at Hardcastle Crags are the most beautiful, extensive woods I know of in this region; and it is one of the victories of the Council for the Preservation of Rural England that they were saved from being flooded to make yet another reservoir. I am told that, when a petition was raised in Hebden Bridge to protest against the planned flooding, only the smallest proportion of Hebden Bridge inhabitants had even been to the woods, let alone were concerned to preserve them.

Certainly people care about them now. Crowds of families picnic there on Sundays and on Bank Holidays—the men lingering under the trees with the melancholy expressions of people undergoing religious conversions; the women seeming to be preoccupied with improperly-left domestic cares, or with ways of restraining the instinctive primitivism of children loosed amongst the trees.

Now the woods have passed to the National Trust; and, as so often when a rural place is preserved as a place of "relaxation", a Boy-Scoutish amateurism affects it. There are toy-like bridges; log cabins; "scenic" benches; petty notices forbidding this and that; a "wishing well"; and a striped barrier, like a frontier post, across the road. The woods are charming, with the charm of a spoilt child; and, like a spoilt child, the coy, cultivated charm is a bit repulsive.

Fortunately, the collection boxes at the roadside don't seem to take money for too many of these park baubles; and the artificial features are easy to get away from.

About a mile into the woods from the Hebden Bridge end is a disused woollen mill—a thorn in the flesh of the National Trust, as it were. This is as far as most visitors, approaching from Hebden Bridge, go. In the row of otherwise derelict cottages by the mill, one is used as a café, open on Bank Holidays and occasional weekends. Here I turned uphill, over the pack-horse bridge; climbed up the green, brilliant slime at the side of a long waterfall; and broke into the sparkling bare fields near Heptonstall.

Walshaw Dean reservoirs were built by Enoch Tempest. He was

born the son of a quarry owner in Haworth in 1843. After a wild
youth, in which he frightened villagers with his drunkenness, he
became a teetotal contract builder of reservoirs. (It is said that,
after one drunken outing, he came-to in New York, and that having
to work his passage home made him teetotal; an alternative is that
he was shipwrecked, and the water sobered him.)

To carry building materials and men to sites high on the moors,
he and his brother James used the new steam-locomotives with
incredible optimism; they gave them affectionate names, like
Minnie and Harold and Annie and Little Egret and Tenacity and
Esau.

He built a reservoir near Keighley and one near Matlock; he
widened the canal in Leicester; then he built Clough Bottom
reservoir, at Windy Bank, 1,000 feet high on the Burnley Road;
and Barley Reservoir, below Pendle Hill, near Nelson. He moved
to live in luxury at Oak Dene near Marple, Cheshire, where for a
hobby he laid out the park with roads and services for building
developments, stipulating that the houses to be built in his park
must cost at least £1,000 each.

In 1900 he submitted the lowest tender to Halifax Corporation for
building a chain of three reservoirs at Walshaw Dean.

The site is between 1,000 and 1,200 feet above sea-level. He
built a group of wooden huts at Heptonstall to house Irish navvies.
This was called Dawson City. From here he built a three-foot
gauge railway for five miles to the reservoir sites. Part of the engineering for this was a trestle viaduct made of pitch pine, 700 feet
long and 105 feet above the stream at Blakedean: the base of the
trestles is still standing. The railway's fifteen locomotives were
dragged from Hebden Bridge station on Saturday afternoons, when
the cart horses of Hebden Bridge tradesmen could be hired to
make up teams of up to sixteen horses that helped steam-lorries
drag the locomotives 400 feet up the hill to the workshops at Dawson
City. Fifteen-year-old horse-tramcars from Liverpool became the
"Paddy Mail" that took the Irish navvies from Dawson City to the
reservoirs at half past five in the morning.

Enoch Tempest was bankrupted by his imagination. After he had built his reservoirs, they leaked, and the shock of losing all his money in trying to repair them brought on a stroke; he died in 1908.

But in one house of a bleak terrace of a dozen houses, flush to the road at Colden, above Heptonstall, lives a ninety-five-year-old man, Charles Chambers, who was the driver of Esau, one of Enoch Tempest's engines.

He walks sturdily; his face is long, large and cadaverous. He wears the jacket and trousers of an engine driver.

"A come up here eighteen year ago to wear me old clothes out," he shouted, because he himself is a little deaf. "Am still here," he added, raising his voice further, as if challenging a dispute. The house is clean and tidy: it's always like that, though his wife has died. On the wall over the kitchen fireplace he is painting a picture. The picture matches the view through the window. A roll of dark green paint is indisputably similar to the side of Stoodley Pike; a roll of more brownish green is the field of rushes immediately beyond the window, before it falls into the deep invisible Calder Valley that lies between here and Stoodley Pike, and whose space is difficult to suggest in such a painting technique as that of Charles Chambers. He has imitated the Stoodley Pike monument by cutting it out of plywood and gluing it above the green. He was painting this view when I visited him a year ago, and layers of paint have been applied since. You can tell from the painting that he is a little short-sighted; but not much.

"I've still got all them walls to do," he said.

Leaning against the pot cupboard is a smaller picture: Esau, very tiny but in full detail, crosses an equally detailed Blakedean viaduct in a vast, less well-observed landscape.

He walked into the front room and paused before the window. Then he expanded his arms, with a gesture of withdrawing the curtains.

"It's grand to look out on in the mornings," he bellowed, as if his voice had still to reach across the Wadsworth Valley.

What delighted him was his garden, which was about the size of two graves, and built into the bank on the other side of the road. Its wooden fence, a foot high, and its gate of the same height, were painted with thick encrustments of paint in cream, and brick red, and dark green.

Within the fence, lining the pebbled paths eight inches wide, were clipped bushes a few inches high that stood as trees to a model village, church and cottage and pub, built out of plywood, divided also by tiny pebble-stone steps. In the corner of the garden a five-foot high pole carried a curious wooden thing, part model aeroplane, part model windmill, that whirred and twisted in the wind. In the centre of the garden was a plaque, which said: "What will our harvest be."

6

When I left Charles Chambers, I walked along the ridge of that high spur of land, separating two wooded valleys, and at the end of which is the stony village of Heptonstall. High as it is, it is difficult to see across the country; black stone walls close one in—a suitable preparation for the close walls of Heptonstall. From Heptonstall, I dropped steeply downhill again to the Calder Valley.

A bus conductor once told me that there are people who, on sunny days, board the bus in Halifax, sit on the top deck, and travel the thirteen miles or so to Todmorden and back, so as to restore themselves by taking what is called "a breath of fresh air".

But that stretch—or any stretch—of the Calder Valley is not where most people would go for such an outing.

I know, also, someone who, after I'd given him an idea of West Yorkshire as a place of moorland spaces, waterfalls and clear streams, came to visit me, but travelled that same bus route, and returned to London immediately, in disgust. His reaction was, perhaps, more typical.

On the map the Calder Valley is represented by a black, knotted, hairy line laid casually across apparently nameless and unmarked spaces. The Calder Valley is in fact a tightly intertwined thread of road, railway, canal and greasy river confused with undivided industrial villages and towns. Where the valley is narrow there are connected villages hemmed in by the tall banks of the moors. Wherever there is a space—that is, wherever a tributary joins the Calder, forming a small, triangular shallowness in the land— there is as big a town as the space will allow: thus arose Rochdale and Littleborough (where apparently the same river is called the Roch); Todmorden; Hebden Bridge; Mytholmroyd; Sowerby Bridge; Elland; Brighouse; Mirfield; Dewsbury; and Wakefield, until the Calder becomes a tributary of the River Aire, east of Leeds.

The valley is one long, continuous but confusingly mixed, neglected museum of our industrial history. Grand, Tudor houses like Kilnhurst, different to Tudor houses in other parts of England in having a third storey with a continuous line of small windows along their walls—these windows are called weaving lights, and were to let as much light as possible into workrooms where cloth was woven—are shabby and neglected, unwanted because of their position amongst nineteenth-century mills that still seem like temporary camps in their parks. Here and there are neon-lit successes that seem boastful amongst the more numerous mills that are closed, not wanted for any purpose at all, but are still in the valley because it would cost too much to demolish them; or, if they're still used, they seem quaint and precarious with their huge stone walls buckled like cardboard—as is Maude's Clog Works at Mytholmroyd.

The River Calder is, they say, one of the hardest worked rivers in England. There are few places where the arteries of water are allowed their natural flow. Everywhere, it is carefully conserved: water flowing from the millstone-grit hills was the most important factor to the woollen industry. Travelling here in 1750, Daniel Defoe noticed how the water was cared for, because it was used in wool-processing. He had been alarmed by his crossing of barren moorland; then:

the nearer we came to Hallifax, we found the houses thicker and the villages greater in every bottom; the sides of the hills which were very steep every way, were spread with houses, and that very thick; for the land being divided into small enclosures from two acres to seven acres each, seldom more; every three or four pieces of land had a house belonging to it.

Then it was I began to perceive the reason and nature of the thing, and found that this division of the land into small pieces and scattering of the dwellings was done for the convenience of the business which the people were generally employed in——This business is the clothing trade.

We could see that almost at every house there was a tenter and almost on every tenter a piece of cloth, or kersie, or shalloon.

As our road passed among them, wherever we passed any house we found a little rill or gutter of running water . . .

Without the same activities taking place (you will now more often see people altering doorways, putting in bay windows, erecting a garage or converting an outhouse—it's as if that is the new cottage industry) the description of the landscape, seemingly overcrowded with small-holdings, is as accurate today as it was in 1750. The tiny streams, the rills forcing their way between stones and grass, spilling through walls, worming from trough to trough, and making such marvellous music on a still night, are still there. There are at least three sulphur springs along the Calder Valley: springs of "spa water" that have been the focus for May Day ceremonies. One is near North Dean Chapel in Luddenden Dean—there is a story that, beginning on Spa Sunday (1 May) in 1890, a patch of whitewash mysteriously appeared on a stone above the spring every year before the festival, and no one discovered who regularly placed it there. Another spring gives its name to Spa Wood in Mytholmroyd. The third sulphur spring is at Simm Carr, Shibden, Halifax. Halifax Temperance Society used to gather here on Spa Sunday to preach the virtues of drinking water; following them, the Labour Party used to remember the first Sunday in May by meeting here.

Other than spa-water springs, the mark of the past importance of the troughs of water is their careful inscriptions. For instance, one in the Dean Head Valley is inscribed: "1829. This trough is the property of C. Reckaby, Esq. and R. Parkinson, the tail of the water to be enjoyed by T. Riding and his house."

In the valleys, the water is diverted through stupendously walled cuttings and dams, directed under mills for a hundred yards, tangled with bridges of various ages, and controlled by sluices. In apparently wild woods, as in the woodlands at Millbank, you are likely to come across magnificent falls over stone walls built to marshal the streams, and across wild overgrown pools and ditches that are the remains of utilitarian diversions of the water.

The woollen industry, that made such demands on the streams here, was once monolithic; combined with the character moulded by Methodism, it was a source of that rigid pride recognizable as "Yorkshire". Now, at best, it has broken down into specialities— trousers in Hebden Bridge; riding clothes in Mytholmroyd—or its buildings are adapted to other uses. Along this stretch of the Calder Valley it is poultry. Amongst the mills are long, sinister sheds with their windows darkened. For a few years, outlying places off the Calder Valley were also notorious drug-growing places.

From the Calder Valley are side valleys that trickle into places that now seem so desolate, one is amazed that they were ever named. But they do have names, which are pagan, like Sun Hill; or Roman, like Rom Hill; or Saxon, like Luddenden (which means "loud water"—and you still hear the water pouring over its rocks, wherever you are in the village); or their names are brutally candid, like Cold Edge, Friendly and Stoney Royd; or they are memorials to an almost forgotten biblical culture—Abel Cross, Jerusalem Farm and Mount Tabor, which are the names of deceased people, or of unused or hardly-used chapels.

7

LIKE WALES, West Yorkshire is now unimaginable without its chapels. The mill and the chapel dominate every village—the first, because of its immensity and its severity; the second, because of its size also (often not so much smaller than the mill) and also because of its symbolically lofty position. Funereally black, like great stone coffins, the chapels crown the hilltops, or at least the most commanding heights in the villages, each one like a memento mori.

Both mill and chapel are starkly utilitarian, despite Greco-Roman excrescences, and a surrounding of gilded or black-painted iron-work. It is clear that the same impulse, the same people, created both.

The chapels are so many, and they are so vast, that one is impressed and amazed at what must have been the sizes of their congregations; one wonders what reasons there were for these gloomy buildings being necessary to the people. How did these chapels come to be?

By all accounts, the Chapel movement began here when that terrible northerner (born in Blackburn), the Anglican curate of Todmorden, William Grimshaw—"Parson Grimshaw"—with his family's reputation for slaying dragons (it is recorded that his ancestor slew a dragon in a Blackburn wood; hence the griffin on the Grimshaw arms, and on pub signs in that district); with his notorious horse whip which he used for driving drinkers out of the pubs and into church; with his implacable conviction and with the avenging sword of his rhetoric ("he feared no man but himself") —was converted from Anglicanism to Methodism.

Perhaps there was something sado-masochistic about this man. He swung from the blackest visions, despair and the contemplation of suicide, to the most jubilant, euphoric states. He once stopped in mid-sermon to pronounce, "My friends, we are all in a damnable state, and I scarcely know how we will get out of it". When his first wife died (he outlived two of them; the second one died of a fever raging through Haworth whilst Grimshaw was incumbent there) he made the most morbidly detailed and also comic plans for his own funeral:

To a funeral sermon	10/6
To church dues	5s.
To a horse litter	£1 1s.
To a coffin	£1
To 2 gallons of claret	6/8
per gal., 5 qts at home, 3 qts at drinking house	
To 20 2 penny cakes	3/4
To 20 penny rolls	1/8
To 25 pairs of gloves	£1
To expence of inviting to funeral	3s.
To parson and clerk each a penny cake and other odd.[1]	

Then, after his conversion—which is said to have been after a Scotsman converted to Evangelism, a shoemaker and pedlar named William Darney, appeared at Heap Farm, about a mile and a half from Bacup on the road to Todmorden, and preached there, thus beginning the first of his "Darney Societies"—Grimshaw's attitude seems to have been equally unrealistic, and elevated to another extreme.

"I was now willing to renounce myself," he said, "and to embrace Christ for my all in all. O, what light and comfort did I now enjoy in my soul, and what a taste of pardoning love of God."[2]

And when he actually was dying, he is supposed to have said

---

[1] Cragg, *Grimshaw of Haworth*, Canterbury Press, 1947.
[2] Ibid.

"I have nothing to do but to step out of my bed into Heaven, I have my foot on its threshold already."[1]

His energy was enormous. In 1743, after he became minister of Haworth, he started twelve meetings for prayer and worship in cottages scattered distantly over the intractable moorlands of his parish. In bad or good weather, he walked or travelled by horse over the moors to small numbers of people gathered in these cottages. He preached twelve to fourteen times in what he called a "lazy week" and twenty to thirty times in a busy one.

Looking at his engraved portrait in the *Methodist Magazine* for 1821—at that solid, well-fed face, with its assertive eyes, its cleft chin, its well-mannered wig, and only the pouting, cherub lips, to show him, perhaps, as something other than a businessman, worldly-successful through his ruthlessness—it is difficult to realize that there was also something theatrical about him. Parson Grimshaw, who once wore a horned mask to impersonate the Devil and frighten a young man into marrying a girl whom he had seduced, was ruthless with such theatrical devices when, as a Methodist, he fought the Devil. He came to be called "Mad Grimshaw" and the legend was evidently useful to him. His theatricality was important to his success; and both his success and his theatrical sense of timing and of *le mot juste* are shown in the anecdote about his summons to the Archbishop of York to explain why he attended the Conference of Methodists in Leeds in 1749:

"How many communicants did you find on coming to Haworth?" his lordship asked.

"Twelve, my lord."

"How many have you now?"

"In winter, between three and four hundred, according to the weather. In summer nearer 1,200."

"We can find no fault in Mr Grimshaw," said the archbishop, "seeing he is instrumental in bringing so many to the Lord's Table."[2]

[1] Ibid.   [2] Ibid.

There were twelve communicants to the church at Haworth when Grimshaw came; before he had finished, there was an occasion when 6,000 people came to hear Charles Wesley preach there.

"Members of Darney's new formed societies at Millers Barn, and at other places, used to walk twenty miles to attend the ministries of Grimshaw at Haworth. Their route was . . . over hills some of which were 1,500 feet above sea-level, across deep and rugged valleys; but their new-born zeal surmounted all difficulties."[1]

"What hath God wrought in the midst of these rough mountains," Wesley wrote.

All the ingredients of "God's" success, repeated through many preachers, are in Grimshaw's career. Beginning with Grimshaw, Methodism began its 200-year reign over the yearnings for solutions and answers that only religion can provide; and over the hysteria and confusion of West Yorkshire people caught in a social change.

With its colourful, apocalyptic oratory, and its "conversions" it also satisfied the need for something that is both entertaining and elevating—since the demise of the numerous Nonconformist churches, the same need has drawn groups of thousands to listen to and to participate in pop music. And, just as enormous demand has caused the pop-music cult to differentiate itself into a variety of groups representing different facets of itself, so, in order to cope with its swarms of converts, the Nonconformist Church differentiated itself into marginally differing groups—Whitfield's Calvinistic Methodists; the New Connexion; the Unitarians; the Baptists; the Congregationalists; the Primitive Methodists.

Like pop singers; like Jesus and his disciples; like medieval troubadours; Nonconformist preachers gained part of their glamour by being, at one and the same time, mysterious travellers, pregnant with untested promise, who appeared to reject ordinary values of human success and yet who flashed a most enviable, rare success through their oratorical powers. They were almost (but, enticingly, not quite) palpable; they were (almost) touchable symbols of freedom

[1] J. W. Laycock *Methodist Heroes of the Great Haworth Round, 1734–1784*, Wadsworth Co., 1909.

from the clay of our bodies and of our ordinary mean desires, who, in their persons, proved success; their words could actually be heard, the dress and manners of such a free person could actually be seen.

Almost, they were sacrifices, too, who were encouraged to do without the normal comforts of settled life, in order to represent the otherwise unmanifested, noble parts of their followers.

In using his horse whip to drive drinkers into church; in being permitted, in being even encouraged, to do this, Grimshaw was a sacrifice to a super-human world, where he must behave as no other human is allowed to behave, and be lonely in it for the sake of what he represents of others.

God's surrogate in West Yorkshire created a religion that in some ways was releasing, but in other ways was a terrible doctrine of "thou shalt not". It was a religion that forbade so much—drinking; dancing; music other than that accepted as being directly in "the service" of God; painting; and anything other than the narrowest sexuality.

One way to enforce its terrible sobrieties was to point out how awful it would be if, having failed miserably in life, as most people did, you were then to enter an eternal life in Hell because you had died without the Gospel in "your heart". As alternative, the Church offered its eternities of, presumably, something like being in church— something clean; dry; sacramental; resounding with intoxicating words; and smelling of furniture polish.

It also seemed to prove that, in any case, to accept its "thou shalt nots" was an indispensable element in temporal success, at a time and in a place where the price paid for not being one of the worldly-successful few was that frightful, grovelling hardship of the many. "Methodists in every place grow diligent and frugal, consequently they increase in goods," wrote Wesley. As K. S. Inglis writes in his *Churches and The Working Class in Victorian England*:

In 1856 the historian of a flourishing Methodist circuit declared that many a rich man would have been still in squalid poverty

F

if Methodism had not taken him by the hand. "It was she that saved him from rags—put him on his feet—gave him a character, and placed him in the path of industry in which he has found both affluence and position."

In West Yorkshire in the nineteenth century, when it could be seen that so many were making large fortunes very quickly, it must have seemed that the way to become as they were was to do as they did—that is, to attend chapel.

Farm kitchens, like those at Hardibutts Farm and at Cross Ends Farm, in Crimsworth Dean above Hebden Bridge, were opened for services; cottages and barns were adapted as chapels, before money could be raised by subscription to build them.

The Baptist collier, Dan Taylor, himself quarried the stone, and almost by himself built Heptonstall Methodist Chapel.

Dan Taylor was responsible for the revival of the General Baptists in Yorkshire, and he is a typical example of the self-taught man in the great age of self-help. He was working in the pits at the age of five and remained a miner until adolescence, when he came under the influence of the Methodist Revival; he then turned preacher after withdrawing from the Methodists on points of order and doctrine, and became convinced of the rightness of Baptist principles. Unable to obtain baptism from the local Particular churches, he set off on foot for the nearest General Baptist Church known to him, in Lincolnshire, and was baptised, out of doors, in February 1763. He returned to Wadsworth and set up a church, the meeting house for which he worked at with his own hands——He spent his time teaching himself, keeping a shop and a farm, to support his large family, but all the while attending to a vast amount of pastoral work.[1]

The absolute determination, overcoming all difficulties, over-

[1] Frank Beckwith, "The Old Dissent" collected in *A History of Christianity in Yorkshire*, F. S. Popham (ed.), The Religious Education Press Ltd.

coming all human need for rest, to build God's mansion!—which, as it turned out, was as bleak as an outcrop of millstone-grit rock; and whose conditions were as harsh, spiritually, as those of a mill were, physically.

There was a fury of building, when the Methodists littered the hillsides with glorious, stark and now unused chapels. The forbidding element in its doctrine was most naturally reflected in the forbidding appearance of its buildings. They were churches without steeples and which rarely carried a Cross, because these were marks of Anglican idolatry; instead they were decorated with abstract patterns and arabesques, or with the texts "God is Love" and "Repent ye for The Kingdom of Heaven is at Hand", and with a clock, a high pew, and a glass of water. They were eclectic buildings in all the fashionable styles of the late nineteenth century—neo-classical; Gothic; art-nouveau; and which smelled of pine, varnish and wax-polish.

In these chapels—and also outside them, in the fields, the factories, and in homes—there was a frenzy of conversion.

In the chapels, the adults, embarrassed by their suddenly discovered guilt and sin before their watching children, "cried to the Lord to save their souls".

One preacher, Isaac Marsden, drew a chalk line across the floor of Mount Tabor Chapel, Halifax, and invited his congregation to either step over the line into eternal life, or "to remain for ever in outer darkness".

A man shouted to his daughter "Come on, Nellie, help me sing, I'm on my way to glory where pleasures never die."

A nailmaker, Jim Melling, was converted whilst he stood on a chair at home. He shouted "I am son of a King." His mother asked if he'd gone out of his mind.

"No," he replied, "I'm coming back to it."

John Turton lived in Horbury and played the fiddle. When he became "convinced of sin" he felt that his fiddle was "a snare of the

Devil that bewitched and threatened to destroy him" and that it "came between him and salvation".

One night, walking the road between Horbury and Dirtcar, he turned this question over in his mind: "Shall it be the fiddle, the public house and the Devil; or Christ, the Chapel and salvation?"

As he thought about this, he saw a flash from a fire of thorns in a field. This seemed to be a sign from God; he jumped the hedge and thrust the fiddle into the fire.[1]

The nation that had won the Battle of Waterloo and was conquering nature so dramatically, particularly in Lancashire and West Yorkshire, saw military analogies in these victories over sin. "Every night, during the crusade, that tiny room became alive with the power of God, as Jim Beesley stormed the gates of Heaven in prayer." Foreign enemies; undisciplined nature; and the inner life of man, were all conquered in that century, it seemed.

> Give me the faith which can remove
> And sink the mountain to the plain

was Charles Wesley's expression of that relationship between the Methodist faith and the contemporary, pragmatic subjugation of nature; his couplet was more accurate than he, perhaps, thought.

In 1899, the Rev. J. Baker Norton wrote in the *Methodist Magazine* of one of these "outpourings of the spirit":

men could not settle to work and it was no unusual thing for the miners, in the bowels of the earth, to lay aside their tools in order that they might hold prayer meetings. . . . Down in the gloom, Heaven's light shone in upon penitent hearts and they became new creatures. . . . In many of the houses and mills the hymns heard in the services were sung daily.

Maybe some of the hymns that were daily sung were these:

[1] These illustrations are taken from *Chapel* by Kenneth Young, Eyre, Methuen, 1972.

Bear with me when I say the crime is great
Of those who practice coming late;
As if God's services were far too long,
So they omit the opening prayer or song.

A little less indulgence in the bed—
A little more contrivance in the head—
A little more devotion in the mind
Would quite prevent your being so behind.

which is from *Stevens Selection*; or one of Sankey's hymns:

I would like to die said Willie, if my
    papa could die too.
But he says he isn't ready, 'cos he's got
    so much to do;
And my little sister Nellie says that I must
    surely die,
And that she and mamma—then she stopped
    because it made her cry.

And maybe one of the hymns that the girls sang at their looms
is this one:

Oh for a man . . .
oh for a man . . .
Oh for a man . . .
sion in the sky!

In a second-hand bookshop, I found a book of *Tales of the West Riding* by F. T. Mormon, which told the story of a hill farmer called Black Sam o' Fieldhead Farm who, made bitter against his wife who had left him, wanted to revenge himself upon her daughter. Turning her out of doors wasn't enough for him, because then she would easily get work as a servant at a neighbouring farm, and probably be happier than she was with her step-father.

So he put a rope round her neck, and sold her in the market. A weaver, who was a widower and had no one to care for his children, bought her for sixpence. She was happy with the weaver and his children, and she became known as "Mary as was selled for sixpence".

Black Sam was discussed by the labourers waiting for hire at the Martinmas Fair; and because he was so misanthropic, no one would work for him.

"What make o' gaffer is Learoyd?" one asked.

"A hard man with a face like beer when thunder's turned it sour. His wife left him and he can't bide with women in the house."

Because of this, and because he had neither wife nor daughter to bully at his farm, Black Sam became lonely.

The pub gave him forgetfulness whilst he was in it; but it did not ease his loneliness when he was alone at night, or when he was working on his farm during the day. So he went to the chapel of the Primitive Methodists.

One day after a service, the preacher got Sam Learoyd and one or two others on their knees, and wrestled with the Devil for their souls.

"I've never seen such a chewing of the spirit since I became Methody," said the preacher. "I kept pleading, 'Tread the old Devil under foot and think on the blood of the lamb that washes our sins away'."

The penitents shouted, "I can't! I can't! He's over-strong for me! I'm bound to smother in Hell's fires!"

But the preacher persisted, until one after another shouted, "I'm saved! I'm saved! I've found the Lord!" and they got up and walked weak-kneed out of the room.

But Sam Learoyd, because of the weight of his sins, found it more difficult.

"Let me be," he said. "If I'm bound to find salvation I'll find it by meself." So the preacher gave up praying and let the Lord settle it in his own way.

Suddenly there was a howling that they thought was the wind;

but it was the groans of Sam Learoyd. The preacher knelt beside him and began to sing "Rock of Ages" softly.

Sam Learoyd's groans stopped. "I'm convicted of sin," he said; and he began to go to chapel twice on Sundays. He also gave up swearing and drinking; and instead of going to the pub he stayed at home and read the Bible.

But his conversion was not complete. He had achieved the conviction of sin; he had repented; but he had not reached a sense of forgiveness and peace. So he was tortured by his sins, and he became ill.

The doctor said that someone must live with him and look after him, but of course no one would go—except his stepdaughter, Mary.

One evening, whilst she was there, Sam Learoyd read the twelfth chapter of *Romans*: "Therefore, if thine enemy hunger, feed him; if he thirst, give him drink; for in so doing thou shalt heap coals of fire on his head."

He began to think that the reason why Mary had returned to look after him was to "heap coals of fire upon his head".

And if she were here only to get her revenge, how then could he turn the tables upon her; how could he outdo her at her own plotting, and heap coals of fire upon her head?

There was only one way. He took the rope that he had used to lead her to market, and he hanged himself.

8

THE RIVER CALDER and its valley sways through Sowerby
Bridge; but the road has developed away from there, to lead you to
Halifax, which has become more important than Sowerby Bridge,
because, beginning with the Piece Hall, it developed as a trading
as well as a manufacturing centre.

The road climbs, between houses now being demolished, to
King Cross, which is on the hill dividing Halifax from Sowerby
Bridge. Amongst the slovenly fall of black houses are two curious
phallic structures. One is the famous Wainhouse Tower. This was
begun as a mill chimney; then, because a neighbouring mill and
landowner objected to it, it was finished off with a decorated top,
a spiral staircase was built inside it, and it became a means of viewing
the surrounding countryside. The other spiky erection is a church
tower and spire that have been cleaned and left standing after the
church it was connected to was demolished, and replaced with a
little park.

Most of the demolition here has been done to widen the road
excessively, and create a traffic bottleneck in Sowerby Bridge. You
will see the extraordinary, divisive difference between an old and a
new town, if you travel along the widened road and over the
motorway and bridge that spans the centre of town: its concrete
towers rise over the old, decorative iron bridge that crosses the
river. Below you, like a toy town, are those old black mills,
looking very tiny.

If, instead of following the grand road into town that passes
between the park (oddly called Peoples' Park) and the erstwhile
homes of the Halifax rich, you cut into the grid-iron of straight
streets to your left, and travel to town that way, you will find a
quite different Halifax. It's a local Soho, with its cosmopolitan
community (many of them Indian and Pakistani; but not entirely

so); its junk shops that sell glittering armouries of blunted swords
and knives, electric gadgets and crockery (close to the windows) and,
in barn-like upper storeys, wardrobes, chests of drawers, chairs,
and beds; the old almshouse, fortified within a high wall, with its
bricked-up cells off a glass-littered space; and its Mackintosh's
sweet factory. Someone told me that the founder of this firm
taught his children a verse as a guide to success in life:

> Early to bed, early to rise
> Never get drunk; and advertise.

At the far end of town, the organization associated in everyone's
mind with Halifax—the Halifax Building Society—has recently
forsaken its marble halls for a vast new building. At the centre of
town is the market.

I've never had much patience for foresight; and although before-
hand I knew it, now I realized how badly equipped I was for a
week's walking. I had many pairs of nearly worn-out trousers; and I
had an ex-RAF jacket that was small for me. My shoes—which were
not designed hikers' shoes, in brown, costing about twelve pounds;
but were a pair of worker's black shoes, exactly like hiker's shoes,
but costing two pounds—were almost worn out. I had a fairly
good hat. A while before I'd seen a fur hat belonging to a friend
who'd been to Moscow; I thought the hat suited me better, but
she wouldn't sell it, and the only one I could find like it I bought in
Oxford Street, London. It was black, and made of nylon fur. But
it had a peak and a high front; an Oxford Street cross between
Russia and the Coldstream Guards. It didn't seem at all odd in
London. But people in the Calder Valley smiled at it, and at the
RAF jacket. I thought I was pretty well suited for a hat; but I needed
to go to the market for some other clothes.

Halifax Market is a remarkable place for such a town. The
architecture of it, for a start—that such beautiful, vast Edwardian
architecture, painted decorative ironwork supporting high arches
of glass, should remain unvandalized by modernization, or even

undemolished, in a northern town! After all, Bradford used to have a market very like the one in Halifax; but Bradford's was recently demolished, despite the usual protests. Halifax Market has stalls selling a most remarkable variety of cheeses, sausages, meats, coffees, which, I guess, remain here after having a rich and discerning clientele in Edwardian days.

I got everything I needed in an ex-Army stores near to the market —a pair of shoes similar to the ones I now threw away; a black PVC coat that made me, with the hat, look, I think, a bit sinister; two Army shirts, without collars (but when I tried them on, the stitching was so awry that the material was pulled in all ways unrelated to human anatomy; I guessed they were the cast-off first attempts by some amateur Army tailor)—the whole lot for seven pounds; and a couple of women gave me a cup of the tea they were drinking in the shop.

Adelaide Shaw lives alone in a small terraced house at Pye Nest, King Cross, Halifax—just below Wainhouse Tower. She is seventy-nine years old. As you can see from her photograph, she was a beautiful girl, with that bold and solid look of most West Yorkshire girls when they are beautiful—here, skinny girls are not usually the pretty ones—and she is beautiful now. Her face has aged in such a way that the lines mostly run vertically down her face, leaving her cheeks so unmarked that they could be the cheeks of a fifteen-year-old girl. Even though her house is one of an estate, over the rooftops she has a view of the Ryburn Valley where she has spent her life.

Repeatedly anxious lest it was of no interest to anyone, particularly "the young", she told me her life story. This is it.

"I was born at a farm up Soyland. My father had a lot of bad luck. He wasn't farming then, he was a paper finisher—they used to count the reels as they came from the mill. He kept going to a job and then something happened so he went to another one and we were moved around quite a bit. In those days a lot of mills were burnt down. That at Ripponden was burnt. When a mill burnt down they couldn't stand around in the village, they had to walk somewhere and get something else. It happened quite a few times and I suppose he got a bit frustrated and he went to America when I was about thirteen. He worked his passage across and only stayed about twelve months. My father farmed from then on, except when he took it into his head he would go and have a fish shop in Halifax up Hanson Lane. It did well, but we used to be open until twelve o'clock at night and standing over this fish shop wouldn't do for my mother who'd always been in the fresh air in the country. My father used to take her for a walk up Hanson Lane every night after twelve o'clock. 'Well this won't do at all,' he says, 'I'll go back to farming.' We started farming again when I was seventeen. We lived at The Breck, and at Red Brink on Crow Hill. Red Brink belonged to the chapel, I don't know whether it had been left to them or something. Most of my mill life was spent up the hillside there. He farmed up at Kebroyd. Then when my mother died we came to live in Halifax and so my husband and I persuaded him to come and live at a cottage up the roadside there. But he always wanted farming and he used to look at his hands and say 'Look at these hands.' We'd say, 'What's the matter with them?' 'Oh I'd rather have a spade in my hands than a fork.' He didn't like retiring. He used to go often to look at the farm when it was rented just to do bits. They only have horses there now. My father would turn in his grave if he knew it was trampled up with riding horses—because he was a dairy farmer, and that was that.

"We used to pay threepence or fourpence a week to go to school. When we left we got so many marks from the teacher to say whether we were fit and intelligent enough to go to work. The men that were the overlookers used to be looking out for girls that were leaving school and two or three asked my mother if I could go and work in their mill. My sister started when she was twelve. I wasn't very strong: I don't know why I had to go in the mill because every

now and then I had to have a month nearly off poorly. I think my
dad realized I wasn't very strong but I don't think it was ever
thought you could do anything else. They were poor and they
needed the money and as soon as they had a worker that was it,
you had to work to bring some money home and so you didn't
think about your health. All our parents ever thought about was
work, work. I don't think they ever left the village, you know.
If my mother went to Halifax she used to think she was going a
long way. She used to bring us a present back of a penny bar—
they were squares of chocolate. But when he went to America my
father did say I wasn't to go in the carding room at the mill on
no account. He said I could go anywhere else but not in the carding
and it did cause a bit of trouble with my uncle, and I went doubling.
That was hot in the doubling but it wasn't the dirt. Carding was
that fluff—it's scrubbing the cotton off. It was a bit like that candy
floss that you buy. But I think it was being confined in the mill
for so long that in the end—but I was twenty-five when I gave up—
my father said: 'Well it seems you're not going to keep it up. It's
going to keep getting at you is the mill.' Funnily enough after that
I've been stronger than my sister.

"It was all new machinery when I went to the mill. It was lovely.
Everything shone, you had to clean it and clean it with white
linen. All the beginners were doffers—they were mugs, like, running
around fetching the bobbins. We used to fill this big basket on
wheels that we called a 'skip' with bobbins and wheel it up to
these long machines and put the bobbins on. We were too small
to reach the machinery so we used to get a piece of wood that we
called a 'broych' that had the cops on so we could reach to put the
bobbins on the machines. The machines were what they called
'ginnies'. The machines used to come together—like that. The space
between they called the 'ginney gate'. You could get through this
little bit when the ginnies were out but if they were coming together
you'd to make a dash for it to get out of the way.

"We started at six o'clock. We had to be up before six and we
worked until half past five and I lived right on the hilltops. We had

to work all the time, there was no breaks. We didn't have a cup of tea in the middle of the morning or anything like that.

"The bosses used to walk up and down. We hadn't to sit down you know. I don't know what they'd think if they had to go back to what we did. There was nowhere to make a cup of tea if you wanted one. We used to take our food packed up. There was nowhere to warm anything. We used to go to the engineer's home and she had a boiler with a tap on it and we used to queue up with our pots, tea and sugar or cocoa and sugar or whatever we were having, then she was stood at a table with a milk jug and a spoon and we paid threepence a week for that.

"You daresn't be late back. The overlooker used to come into the millyard. The first time you were late he'd just go like that!— and look at his watch. He wouldn't speak but it was as bad as nearly saying something to you. We used to creep past him and go in. But if you were late two days together he'd give you a good swearing at and say 'See this doesn't happen agin.' But if it did happen I've known him send them back—and you had to come again at half past eight. And you'd gone there for six o'clock. He was very strict, but he got the work out of them.

"I remember one winter it was snowed up so much that the lane was level. The lane was cut out of the fields; and the fields on top and the lane was filled up with snow and we couldn't get out. It had to be cut out before we could go to work. My brother worked at Thorpe Mill—is it a mill now, Thorpe Mill?—and it was breakfast time before we could get to go to work. There's a lot of broken cars there now, isn't there? He got there at breakfast time and they sent him right back. Right up to the top there! So my father says, 'Right' he says. 'You're not going back.' 'Oh!' he says, 'I'll have to go back, I'll have to.' 'No,' my father says, 'you're not going back. Come along a me.' He went to Sowerby Bridge and got him in at another mill. He went to see them at Thorpe Mill and he says, 'You want to see what this boy went through to get here.' There was no snow in Triangle but it had drifted on the hilltops. Then my brother stayed on at this second mill until he went driving buses. They all came out of the mill when they could. But there's still good money to be made there now, isn't there?

"There wasn't unions in those days . . . until I got older and then they started. Those that were in the union started coming round and asking us and we had to join. Dugdales always did very fair to us. When we did anything wrong we used to choose four to go to the manager in the office. 'Who's going to go?' Well it was a case of 'Will you go and I'll go and I'll go if you'll go with me.' We talked to him and he would come out and look at us and look at the work and we often got satisfaction. We never used to have trouble but if we had bad work we had to see to it that it was put right. Dugdales used to give us a treat once a year. One year it was a double wage and I remember my wage was eight and six for Christmas. Another year they gave us a charabanc outing to More-cambe. The charabanc didn't come and collect us like they would now. We'd to go to the top of Ludden Lane. It was a pouring wet morning and they put this hood up. There was nothing at the side and we were all huddled to the middle because the rain was blowing in but oh! we thought we had a marvellous time when we went to Morecambe for the day. And then another time they gave us a social and dance. We thought that was nice.

"It was a long walk back home from half past five. You were too tired to think about going anywhere else. Mother always had a good dinner for us. We were dirty and wanted a wash, you know —there was nowhere to wash at the mill. And we had to put our food up for the next day. 'Jock' we used to call it—'putting your jock up'. We had a little tin that was divided in the middle, one portion for breakfast and one for tea and sugar and for dinner. My mother wasn't a very strong woman so we tried to help her at nights. We did a lot of the housework. Monday night we had to finish washing socks and dusters and emptying tubs. The men wore white velvet corded trousers and they were scrubbed every week. I remember my mother scrubbing all the clothes on the table. You had two oak tubs and you had a peggy stick with a lot of legs round the bottom. We used to put the clothes through both

of these tubs, back again into the boiler, back again into some
clean water, and when you'd got them dry you turned them through
the mangles again and they were all nicely folded *before* you ironed
them. It must have been hard work for them, mustn't it? On
the Tuesday when we got home we used to do the ironing. On the
Wednesday she'd be baking all day. The baking bowl and all the
dirty utensils were there waiting to be washed. Thursday we had a
fireside full of brasses. It used to take me and my sister an hour to
clean them all. The fender had a right big knob in the centre, where
the rods joined, and we got to arguing so much about who should
clean this knob, we used to do half each. Then my mother would
put an old shawl on the sofa and wrap them all up until Sunday.
On Friday we'd to clean all the windows, mop the flags and clean
the toilet. At harvest time we'd to get our tea and then go working
in the fields until it was dark. When the first world war started me
and my sister had to go round with the milk at weekends standing
on the back of a milk float, not covered up. I don't think we thought
of it as hard work. A lot of people think, oh you were slaves in those
days. But we didn't think we were slaves. It was our life and we
just did it. On Saturdays, we worked until dinner time. It'd be
half past one when we got home. We were so glad sometimes to be
at home and not go into the bottom again. Sometimes at the Sunday
School we used to have a social evening and that wasn't very far.
Sunday was started off with Sunday School at nine o'clock; then
back home, change your dress, and go to church. But we didn't
go out through the week—we were too tired, you know, and then
we lived too far away up on the hilltops and we didn't want to come
down to Sowerby Bridge. We only went to things that were at the
chapel.

"It was the only time we could get dressed up, was Sunday—
only time we got without our clogs. But we only had one Sunday
dress. Your second best would be the one that had been Sunday's
two years before. If you got a nice coat for winter it had to do two
years at least; and the same for a summer coat. You wore up your
old clothes in the mill, and the same for shoes. You only had two

pairs of shoes. I've more pairs of shoes now than I've ever had in
my life. I always wore clogs in the mill but I used to put boots on to
come home. They used to button up the sides nearly to the knee,
and you always carried a button hook with you. I remember having
a pair with twenty-four buttons. We got up half asleep to go
to the mill at half past five in the morning and I used to fasten every
other button because I hadn't time for them all. But it would be
dark and I used to run down that drive to the mill with my every
other button loose.

"If ever we went out we had to be in by nine o'clock every night.
And it had to be nine. It hadn't to be five past. Father always knew
where we'd been. We couldn't just say we were going out; it was a
case of we didn't go out if we hadn't somewhere to go, so we'd
have to tell a white lie probably if we were going somewhere we
shouldn't. In war time they gave dances to gain money to send
parcels to the soldiers and of course we were allowed to go to them
because it was for a good cause. And we would see boys there;
but even then you wouldn't be about with them. You'd be at one
side and the boys would be over there—but of course if they wanted
you to dance they had to come and ask you. But we didn't mix a
lot with them. In those days things were rather too much one way
and now they're too much the other. I don't think they're getting
as much out of life as they could do. It's all for themselves now. I
think they miss the real values when they live just for themselves. I
know living by myself my life was happier at home. I remember we
used to go running up that lane to Red Brink and my brother used
to run faster and say, 'Come on. Put your skates on, it's getting
five minutes to nine'; and I'd say, 'Well I can't run any faster, you
get in first and it'll be alright.' My dad used to look at the clock
if it was turning nine. I remember the first time I went out with
my husband. I was nineteen and it was the Zion Chapel anniversary.
It was a great do then. Zion used to be so full that they put seats
out on the front for people that couldn't get in and seats all up the
sides of the corridors. I used to go to my mother-in-law's for tea—
I was friends with his sister, not with him then—and he brought

me home that night. He said, 'We won't go Triangle way'—you know, down the road—'we'll make our way over the hill.' When we got on the hilltop I said, 'Shall we get there for nine o'clock?' and we ran all over those hills to get back for nine. I remember my sister when she was courting. I had scarlet fever at the time. In those days if you were out of the borough they wouldn't take you away; but you'd to be isolated so they took everything out of one bedroom so it was just bare boards and my bed and a chair for my mother and a little table and I had to stay there for about eight weeks. I was thirteen weeks off work with this scarlet fever. She used to go out in the yard did my sister and look up at the window and tell me all her tales of woe. She was in tears one day. 'I was late home last night and it was only ten past but my father has given it to me. I wouldn't care,' she says, 'I wouldn't care if he'd finished one night but he started again the night after.'

"You know where the Long Chimney is? There used to be a big house there. Is it still standing? We used to ride on the top of the tram so we could look over the big garden. There were some people there called McDougal-Rawsons and every Sunday morning they used to come up in a coach and pair, he in his grey silk top hat and her in all her finery. She was a very fine woman and we used to think it was marvellous because she had such beautiful things and they were nice people. We used to go to the gate about ten o'clock and we used to say, 'We'll see if we can see McDougal-Rawsons coming up', and they used to come up in style and they always waved to us. Like royalty. They used to go up there to church and back and we used to think it was marvellous.

"At Whitsuntide we all walked in the processions. There was no such thing as not walking at Whitsuntide—the little ones first and then the big ones. We used to go to Jerusalem Farm on picnics. There was a place up Bogden called Little London. And there was a little place called New Zealand. We'd set off over the hills and we'd maybe have a shilling or two shillings, that's about all—that was when we were older. When we were younger our mothers would always give us the same as the other girls, sixpence or threepence

G

or whatever it was. If my mother gave us threepence we had to bring some of it back; but she didn't give us less money because she didn't want us to look so poor that we hadn't anything.

"There were some funny folk about then: Grandfather Knock-Em-Off-Top because when he had a pint of ale he used to blow the froth off. He could have been a wealthy man because he had a quarry, but his mouth was too wide. He used to make a lot of money and drink for a fortnight and sleep in his toolshed. Then there was Bull Pratt. He slept in the fields—in a place where there's a rocky road with a stream running down all the time. He slept there amongst the stones and went about in bare feet. And he were a big strong fellow. It took three or four policemen to hold him when they locked him up. And Little Normy: he were a right little fellow but his head and his shoulders and his back looked like an ordinary man's. When he used to get into a pub for a drink he'd sit and his right little short legs were hidden. If he started arguing with any of the other fellars he'd say he could fight them and this that and the other and then when he got down off his seat the fellar nearly fell on his back when he saw what a little un Little Normy was.

"It's a different age now. I wouldn't say anything wrong about it but I think we enjoyed our young days just as much in another way. We perhaps missed out on a lot of things but on the other hand we were kept together a lot more than they are today. We saw each other every day for years and years and at Sundays we'd see some different ones. We'd our Sunday School and we'd our pals there and we'd go for a walk on Sunday afternoons, so I don't think they get much more now.

"We don't say these things because we're frightened that people have got an image of old people going on about the past and they think it's a bore. That's why we don't say anything.

"But we have a laugh when we get together any of us about things we used to do. When we get together we have a real laugh and a real natter; but we don't when there are any young people because we think they're not interested."

Whenever I have been into a mill, what has struck me first of all is the beauty of the light. In some quiet corners—amongst the newly-arrived coils of wool, called "tops", as they wait to be spun and woven; or on the empty, stone stairways—the sunlight lingers in dusty shafts; it is the peaceful, sacramental light of caves and castles and cathedrals. In the weaving and spinning sheds, brilliant fluorescent light is scattered by the movements of machines so rapid that the eye cannot catch them; or it is more sedately reflected from oiled metal; or it makes brilliant the coloured spots of a weaver's scarf or overall amongst the dominant silver of metal and of flying wool; so in the weaving shed the light throbs, flickers, melts, and changes, like the heart of a sunrise.

The tops are like large, white, soft cushions. They unwind gracefully into the machines, seemingly by themselves. Then the noisy hammering begins, as the tops are drawn into fine fibres, and then twisted together, back to their original thickness, but stronger. The threads spread out in their flight through the mill: drawing, finishing, spinning, soft-winding, dying, twisting and steaming, to make it ready for weaving; then warping, weaving, winding, inspection and mending, before it goes to the finishers. So, through room after room, the yarn travels like threads of light through the machines, through the heavy thundering.

In this world, the weavers—like Adelaide Shaw—are the aristo-crats. She is a girl who could have chosen an easier and a better paid job. She could work at "mending", for instance. Then she would sit in a quiet, clean room, and work quite slowly, and chat to her friends, and listen to Radio 1 all day, and not be rushed by remorseless machinery, whilst she checks over the pieces that come from the looms.

But a conviction that she is doing something superior makes a girl become a weaver; and within the weaving shed there is a hierarchy—everyone knows who is the best weaver, who the next best, and so on. To watch a weaver or a spinner working, is to watch someone who seems to be conjuring with light itself. As they are spun off the bobbins, the threads convulse in the brilliant light like electric sparks. To watch a spinner or a weaver joining together two of these writhing threads of light is to watch something that seems like magic. And it seems to be that this manual dexterity of the weaver is a dexterity that she displays throughout her life; so the weaver tends to lead a well-organized life.

I went into Leigh Mills, Pudsey, and watched a spinner working. She was an oldish woman; a "cap spinner"—which is an outdated way of spinning wool, and more difficult than other ways to learn; so now girls are not interested in it. Soon the machines she worked with were to be scrapped; she had been working as a cap spinner in this mill for twenty-seven years, and didn't want to change. She wore carpet slippers and a floral overall; and her way with these vast, noisy, high, banging machines—she, by herself, tended several machines—was as natural and as homely as if she were going about domestic tasks in her own kitchen.

Though she was working with several hundred others in the factory, she was by herself as she worked, isolated by the noise. When they converse, spinners and weavers do it by lip-reading, or by speaking close into one another's ears. As I looked over a room filled with 165 clattering looms, I saw, here and there, these shockingly intimate pairs of girls, apparently kissing one another.

I must have looked awestruck as I watched her sleight of hand with the writhing threads of wool; for as she caught my expression, she laughed. She spoke something, clearly, to me, assuming that I could lip-read. When she realized that I couldn't understand her, she picked up a duster on a stick and began to dust the fluff off the other machine that she tended, and which was now still, and she worked her way towards me as she dusted. When she was close, she shouted in my ear. She wanted to know what I was doing. I told her that I was writing a book.

"I gave 4,000 books to the hospital," she shouted, astoundingly. "My walls are very damp so I had them all in polythene bags behind a curtain in the bedroom. There's not much point in that, is there?"

One of the bobbins on her spinning frame ran out of thread. The empty bobbin spun fiercely. She went to the frame, replaced the bobbin, and knotted the ends of the threads. I tried to catch what she was doing; but I could see nothing more than a changed flicker in the light that was the travelling thread. She came back to shout in my ear.

"I'd rather read than watch television," she said. "People watch television and they want everything they see and it gives them ideas about violence and sex. People are too selfish these days; it's 'dog eats dog' all the time. They're never satisfied.

"Women I know here when they get to my age complain that their husbands aren't as fit as they used to be and can't do as much for them—with me and my husband there's still friendship after sex has finished.

"This country'll never come to anything," she said, "until the women say to their husbands, 'Go out and do some work or there's no dinner nor nothing else.'"

Like most West Yorkshire woollen mills, Leigh Mills had been built in a park, with the mill-owner's house built next to the mill. I could see rooks nesting in the trees; but when I came out of this noisiest of places, the cries of the rooks were muffled and faint, so I wondered if I had damaged my ears, and I shook my head to rid myself of deafness.

9

From Pye Nest I walked downhill to Sowerby Bridge. Sowerby Bridge is like Halifax; in fact, lacking Halifax's grandeur in some pockets of buildings, it seems like part of it. On the right hand side of the main street are some tall, pink, concrete housing blocks that make it look like an Eastern European slum; and a filled-in canal, where an opportunity has been missed to keep at least one attractive walk through Sowerby Bridge. On the left, the land drops more gently to the collection of little yards of small-time engineers and scrap dealers that are often found close to railway lines. But along the main street, and just off it, are several "pie shops": little bakeries, still in business to sell very good quality pies and bread straight from the ovens at the backs of the shops. Their main trade is the same as it's been for a hundred years: they sell cheap, nourishing pies at lunch time to workers from the factories. This time one of them sold pies to a hiker in a funny hat.

I walked out of Sowerby Bridge along that straight road that local lorry drivers call the Long Chimney. There is a tall, black chimney on the right hand side; whether the road is named after that, or whether its name is a metaphor for its straightness, I don't know.

I cut off to the left, past the derelict gardens of the McDougal-Rawsons, into the woods by the river and the old railway line. The river is greasy and grey; it rises only a few miles away, and has only passed through the little village of Ripponden, so it's hard to see why it isn't clean. The mills where Adelaide Shaw worked, as well as other mills, are embedded in the woods. I walked along the cinders of the old railway track, which is still unconquered by grass; after a mile or so I cut uphill, towards Norland.

At Norland is a moor rather different to other moors in Yorkshire. Its plateau has a long fringe of rocks that are only about a hundred yards beyond the road that runs below them; possibly because of the proximity of these decorative rocks, there are the relics of a half-hearted attempt to colonize Norland Moor as a holiday place. In quite a few of the fields are caravans; some of the caravans are converted tramcars, very neglected, and perhaps too rotten to interest the museums where you would expect to find such things.

I climbed on to the top of the rocks. There's a great piece of common land, interlaced with paths. I crossed it until I came to thin oak woods on the other side. Because it is common land, there are fewer of those nineteenth-century walls across it; this, and that most unusual thing in West Yorkshire—oak woods on a hilltop—make Norland Moor a most unusual, spacious, pre-industrial space.

On the other side of Norland Moor I made towards Mr Nicholls' mill.

Mr Nicholls' mill stands alone in the fields on the left of the road as you go from Greetland to Barkisland.

Opposite, for about a mile, the roadside is scattered with grey, stone, competitively neat and mostly semi-detached houses. They have car driveways; front-window exhibits of craftshop pottery and glass; and gardens in which crazy paving and roses are a fashionable lay-out.

You can see little more than some of the roof of the mill, because the yard is filled with twelve-foot high stacks of chairs and benches and wooden filing cabinets and baskets. So much timber—mostly flooring out of demolished mills—is stacked against its walls that you would most likely guess that the kids from those houses over the road are getting stuff ready for Plot Night; and if it's a long time to the 5th November, you'll think that explains why they've been able to gather the biggest bonfire that you've ever seen in your life.

Inside, where two people haven't space to pass one another between the packed banks of leather, fifteen feet high and thirty feet deep, Mr Nicholls, in his Gannex mackintosh, and his assistant Mr Moore, in his tattered Burberry, were moving a heavy bench, its unplaned timbers strongly jointed, and darkened with the stains of spilled oil.

They had unloaded it off a cart in the road, edged it through a high narrow gully between the warped and rain-bleached chairs and the rusting filing cabinets and burst baskets, and into the mill door through an awkward right angle. By this door, timbers that had been rested temporarily had become more permanent when a blackbird nested on their top. Mr Moore had positioned a piece of plywood about the nest, to protect the nestlings and the sitting bird from the sun. Mr Moore and Mr Nicholls edged the old, solid bench as delicately as if it were a set of china cups, round the sitting bird. The mother bird sat tight, tense and bold; I could see her yellow beak, pointing bright as a gun out of the blackness of her body and of her nest.

Now Mr Nicholls and Mr Moore paused, and calculated. They were going to pack this table where Mr Nicholls gauged, expertly, it would fit, in between a hanging cluster of iron paraffin flares, each one as brightly yellow as the blackbird's beak, and a dozen or so baths and sink-tops.

The interior of this mill is as familiar to Mr Nicholls as, say, the inside of a locket containing a picture of her lover is to a love-sick girl; or as the interior of the bedroom is to a person long bed-ridden. Speaking less fancifully, Mr Nicholls says he has "a mental picture of it all, going around everyday looking for something for somebody".

The bench—too clumsy and ugly to have in a kitchen or domestic interior, too low to be useful as a workbench, weighing perhaps two or three hundredweight, taking these two men a morning to manœuvre it into a position from which, should anyone ever want it, and be willing to spend another morning removing it—was worth, perhaps, £1.

Though they worked together familiarly, for they have been together for many years, they addressed one another as "Mr Moore" and "Mr Nicholls", as they discussed the past and possible uses for the bench.

"I think those bolt holes situated in a four be four base signify its use as some type of a base for a machine lathe, Mr Nicholls," said Mr Moore.

The confidence in his voice was a little put-on, a little self-conscious. He is really much less self-assured than Mr Nicholls, because Mr Nicholls is much more often right about such things.

"I think you'll find it's held a tank for paraffin or maybe for diesel oil somewhere, Mr Moore," Mr Nicholls replied.

I walked down the long passageway of the mill. I have learnt not to fear that these high piles might tumble down, for they are most skilfully packed.

"Good morning, Mr Nicholls."

"Good morning, Mr Hughes."

"Good morning, Mr Moore."

"Good morning, Mr Hughes."

Mr Nicholls is a compulsive, nervous smoker of Capstan double-strength cigarettes. He lodged the bench momentarily, so that he could offer one of his cigarettes to me.

"Are you looking for anything in any special line?" he asked. "Or just looking around?"

I think I'm slightly privileged at Mr Nicholls'; I think it's not everyone whom he allows to roam freely through his store—because some people are thieves; and some people are pyromaniacs. Someone breaks into his place once a year, on average. "They are usually proper methodical industrial burglars," he says. Many of these burglaries, he thinks, are committed by scrap-dealers; they call upon him six times a year, not, he thinks, to buy anything, but mostly to see what he has and where he keeps it, so that they know where to look and what to look for when they return, maybe in the night, with a lorry. Recently there have been many small fires locally (two of them at Mr Nicholls' mill) started by a local boy who came with a carrier bag filled with wood shavings and a bottle of paraffin, and then sat on the hillside to watch the burning of hen sheds, carpenters' shops, and mill yards.

"I'd just like to have a look round, Mr Nicholls. To see what's new," I said.

"Yes, thank you, very good": Mr Nicholls paused. "A very useful bench for someone with a greenhouse," he said. "Put plants on it. Very unusual to have a bench as long as this. I think it's held a diesel tank or something in its life."

"I don't have a greenhouse," I said.

"No. Thank you."

"I was wondering if you had any of those doors left," I said.

"Thank you," said Mr Nicholls. "I'll tell you what size they are in a moment. Yes, thank you."

He took out his spectacles' case and pulled from it a piece of a cigarette packet with the sizes of the door written upon it. He has little notes to himself everywhere; telephone numbers on pieces of timber which, in consequence, may not, and probably never will be, moved; and cryptic directions written on withering paper pinned to the doors. These notes are, apparently, hoarded as obsessively as the major items of his trade—as the stacks of rotting leather with the sickening smell that blows hotly out of the building when you open the door.

For Mr Nicholls is really a great collector. Because he is less interested in selling than he is in collecting, it is impossible to bargain with him. He would just as soon keep his goods as sell them; besides, his natural shyness makes the brutality and bullying of bargaining unnatural to him. His wife says that his mother was a "hoarder", "saving bits of string and jam jars because they'd come in for jam making in the summer time". Though his wife tries to resist them, his collections enter his home. For instance, because one night he ran out of cigarettes, he has little caches of packets of cigarettes about the house—one packet hidden in the pocket of his best suit; one packet under linen in a drawer, etc.

"They're a standard fitting for a door," he said, "six foot two by three foot six." Then he corrected himself: "Just a bit bigger than standard."

It didn't really matter; how could I carry doors with me, anyway! But I feel easier if I'm there with an excuse.

"I'll just have a look round," I said.

"Yes. Thank you, Mr Hughes."

Feeling complimented, I moved off to "have a look around".

When he left school, Mr Nicholls worked as a clerk. Then he was apprenticed to a cabinet maker. "I thought I'd be a furniture king," he says.

In two years he had meningitis. The doctor blamed the dust from the sandpaper and the wood, but Mr Nicholls thinks "it was some germ I picked up from the sea on a holiday to Southsea when I was twenty-one".

Indecisively, Mr Nicholls sold vacuum cleaners for a year. Then he entered his uncle's Dickensian office amongst the cloth-traders in the Halifax Piece Hall. "This was what was known as the waste leather trade"—they collected off-cuts of leather from local tanneries, graded them into different qualities, thicknesses, lengths and "square-size measure" and sold them, mostly for saddlery, but also on a stall at Huddersfield Market.

Eventually Mr Nicholls had his own mill, which he converted into a tannery, and where he made belting for machinery in Lancashire cotton mills. When the mills changed to using rubber and canvas V-belting, Mr Nicholls began to lose his trade; and he lost it almost entirely in the 1950s, when the government subsidized cotton-mill owners to scrap their machinery.

At that date, whilst still keeping a small leather trade through buying second and third grade leathers which he sold for making clogs and aprons, the neighbours at those inscrutable houses over the road began to write letters to the local paper and to the clerk of the Council in which they complained of the unsightliness of the mill which Mr Nicholls was stocking with the stuff he was buying at Lancashire mill auctions.

He didn't buy looms, because they were scrap; and he, proudly, is not a "scrap chap". He bought small engineering equipment, the weft and yarn boxes, the baskets and skips, the office and canteen equipment, and the stuff that ascends to mill attics—the stores of house furniture, Victorian and Edwardian clothes, books and out-of-date pictures that mill owners and mill managers store there.

The neighbours spoke to Mrs Nicholls in the streets and in the shops.

"What's he doing with that unsightly rubbish over there?" they asked; "When's he going to stop?"

They might well ask. For several years, Mr Nicholls went to two mill closures each week; he reckons that he visited about 600 auctions. Mr Nicholls, obsessed, had found his vocation.

This is one of the parts of England where the population diminished, between the 1851 census and the 1960s. The Calder Valley prospered so much in the 1850s, and the little farmsteads on the hilltops flourished to provide the towns in the valleys with food, and to provide the cotton and worsted mills high up on the streams with children as labourers; so its collapse from that date onwards is more dramatic, its decline more sordid.

There are hamlets and villages—like Wycoller, near Nelson; and Heptonstall, in the Calder Valley—which the villagers deserted entirely, or almost entirely.

They were deserted, but not demolished; and only a change of interest during the 1960s saved us from these ghost towns. Turning these spent rural acres into suburbs for the cities beyond the Pennines has partly replenished the population, but not sufficiently—yet—to rid them of their dereliction.

Wycoller is, now, a hamlet that is quite empty. There is an empty, windowless stone shell of an Elizabethan hall—Wycoller Hall, which is thought to be the original Ferndean Manor of Charlotte Brontë's *Jane Eyre*—and the shells of a farmhouse, outbuildings, cottages, barns. (Although, as I write, Lancashire County Council—which bought Wycoller in 1890, with the intention of flooding it and building a reservoir—is planning to restore it as part of its plans for a county park.)

In Heptonstall, though people have come back to that claustrophobic village street on the crown of a bleak hill, you can clearly see what they had in mind when they left—there is still the raw-looking housing estate, bigger than the village but on its fringe, and to which they moved. So although the pubs are still open in the village, they are mostly for visitors or for newcomers; and the villagers' own social centre, the Working Men's Club, is a barracks-like building on the opposite edge of the housing estate to the village.

The habit of abandoning, rather than destroying and rebuilding, is quite peculiar, and is evidently a tradition. In Heptonstall, you can see something that I've not seen anywhere else in England. At the end of the nineteenth century, the church roof was damaged in a storm; so it was deserted, and it still stands, roofless in the centre of the village, surrounded by and containing rank grass, and left to collapse at its own organic rate whilst the villagers worship in the Victorian church built in the original graveyard.

Industrial society in West Yorkshire has broken down into huge dumps in requisitioned quarries, or in old mill buildings, like that of Mr Nicholls; and the traditional acceptance of untidy surroundings—"where there's muck there's brass"—seems to have made it easier for local councils to be more untidy than they might be in their clearance of old houses and mills. It has doubtless made the depositing of smaller things in conspicuous places much easier, too—shattered furniture, particularly mattresses and sofas, is a common sight at the sides of moorland roads.

As with most things, there is a living to be made, by some, from this breakdown. Above Luddenden, in the Calder Valley, is a group of quarries being filled with waste tyres—the quarry owner makes a charge per lorry load for dumping there. When a quarry is filled, he covers it with soil; but until then, the sight of piles of tyres a hundred feet high on a derelict hillside is surreal. And at Siddal, above Halifax, is a quarry filled with old aeroplanes, and sections of second-world-war bombers and fighters.

It is possible to live here like an inland beachcomber, picking up what the great grey mills and the depopulated towns have cast

off or unknowingly lost. I have a friend who, living in two neighbouring buildings, an ex-chapel and an ex-school—themselves
things cast aside from their first function—has found it easiest and
cheapest to furnish his huge buildings through this kind of beach-
combing: a set of drawers that once filled out the sides of a chemist's
shop; the boardroom table that once accommodated twenty people
at Co-Operative Society meetings; an out-of-date juke-box. He is
a consumer of non-consumer goods. In his Lilliputian style, he has
been known to go out for a tin of peas for his wife, and instead of
returning in ten minutes, to come home at the end of the morning
from a bankruptcy sale where he had spent twenty pounds on a lorry
load of tinned food that would last them through the winter. When he
asked his children where they would like to go for a birthday treat,
they said "the corporation tip".

Jimmy Nicholls' mill, swamped by its mass of timbers, is like
something that some great tidal wave has swept up out of the towns,
and then retreated from. His vocation, of collecting this around him,
does not seem a peculiar one here.

10

SOMEWHERE, AMONGST THESE valleys that thread their dismal way into Huddersfield, or (romantically) at some "cosy moorland pub", I had to find shelter for the night. I was not far from my deserted, derelict home, and I could have cut back and squatted in it. But that would have been a failure. One thing I had never explored about my own home-place was the shelter available at dusk.

I walked up the road from Greetland, looking a little enviously at the plots of fairy-tale bungalows that break out of the pastures at the roadside; and I thought about my problem, and about these bungalows. Their sacraments of lighting lamps; of sitting down to dinner (I could watch them through their panoramic windows, as if they were public exhibitions); of having baths (I watched the frosted windows glow softly); had suddenly grown distant from me. I was a tired animal, loping through the herbage at the fringe of the moor.

With areas of brick aesthetically balanced against areas of stone, with "Georgian" bow windows and "chalet-type" gables (meaning that the timbers forming the triangle of the gable drooped at their extremities), each bungalow seemed idiosyncratic; each then be-came an absurdity, as I saw a dozen or so bungalows, exactly the same, in a weedy field with a ragged stone wall around it. I saw in each one the same bits of tortured glass, of tortured brass.

I tried to understand why it was that people want to have homes like this. I think there is something dominatingly female about these bungalows, and also something childish. They are fantasies; maybe they are the embodiments of visions and ambitions manufactured by illustrators of fairy stories. Maybe they flatter the dreams planted in girls' minds by Walt Disney, by Cinderella, and by sentimental Christmas cards.

The last of these chalets were clustered around a black, huge mill, the thoroughness and stability of its building a reproach to the flimsy bungalows. Then the pastures and the farms became increasingly neglected as I ascended the moor. Around me was the Yorkshire night: the peculiar West Yorkshire country night, that is not particularly scented, with blossoms, or with the droppings of animals, or with damp earth, or with earth impregnated with centuries of manure, as are other rural places; but which is rich in its sounds. The night bore the noises of factories, which were mostly incessant, quiet knockings, steady as the dripping of a tap, with an occasional loud burst of noise—a jet of steam bursting, or steel sheets dropping on to a factory floor—played against the constant murmur of the wind; a rattling sound as it moved through dry grass stalks. Other sounds entered; a curlew's cry, repeated cuts of sound, sharp as a razor; and the music of streams. Before the sound of one stream faded behind me, another stream was growing louder as I approached it. I travelled through a rising and falling scale of delicate music, that reached out of the moors which were black walls whose curved tops floated under a gentle grey sky where a few stars darted out for seconds and then were doused under invisible clouds. On my horizon, the night sky was coloured by unnatural things. One way, a lurid orange spread from street lamps on to the undersides of clouds; the other way down the valley, I could see a dark mass of foggy cloud approaching like a sticky fluid.

I remembered how, after staying for a few months in a city, what had made me want to live here again was going to Heptonstall at night, and in the darkness feeling, about me, not the close and un-mysterious brilliance of streets, but these vast, imponderable valleys, with lights scattered over their bottoms like a brilliant sediment; and it was sensing, through hearing alone, the life that is about one on the moors in the dark—a restless curlew; or the scream when two invisible shrews met in the grass; or the far barking of a dog, its harshness mellowed by distance; or geese; or the clank of a bucket; or a distant factory pulsing; or the streams.

But I cut away from the open moor; maybe what I wanted was

out there, but I feared what my fate might be. I began to struggle
along the lacings of little lanes, many of them gas-lit though there
are apparently no communities using them much, that fringe the
moor, and whose scatterings of hardly necessary lights give the
impression of a heavily populated city. I ascended and descended
those forbiddingly well-engineered paths, called "snickets", that
link the lanes together. They are firmly cobbled, they have high
firm walls, they are often gas-lit, and they go for miles, through fields
and woods, apparently with little purpose. They are different to
paths in other parts of England, because in other places footpaths
are usually old, pre-industrial routes to churches, and the paths
spread out like wheel-spokes from the parish church; here, the centre
of the paths is more often a mill, and the paths were for the workers
travelling to and from moorland hamlets, and they were built as
thoroughly as the mills were built. You might think that they were
so high-walled to keep agile sheep out; you might think they are
another example of Yorkshire excessive thoroughness. But mostly
they were built by out-of-work weavers in the 1830s, employed by
the parish councils under a cunning system whereby, in order to
receive poor-rates, the councils forced them to work on the roads.
Thus, they were kept out of the mischief that they might have got
into had they had time to think and to organize themselves; and
work was drawn from them at even lower rates of wages than they
were paid in the mills.[1] Each high weighty stone that I passed was
raised in God-knows what misery.

Somewhere—I have no notion of where, in that darkness—I
stumbled on to a pub, dramatically over-lit on an empty road. The
bright lights in the forecourt threw shadows in the opposite direction
to the way sunlight would throw them over the pale paint, so that
the front of the pub was like a clown's mask.

I went inside. The Snug and the Tap Room had been "knocked-
through", as they say. I swung the feeble hardboard doors, and was

[1] "For two days a week roadwork in Saddleworth the weavers received
12 lb. of oatmeal per day." E. P. Thompson, *The Making Of The English
Working Class*, Gollancz, London, 1963.

H

in a large room where the whips, daggers, manacles, and frightful polished chains and harnesses lit by crafty lighting made it ominously like a brothel; otherwise, the style of this blitzed interior was that of an international airport. There was a long padded bar. A tape-recorder played inoffensive music. The structure was mostly concealed under very modern materials—wood and stone reproduced photographically, or imitated in polystyrene; despite this, over the bar a fake-Gothic parchment outlined the history of the building that "went back to the fourteenth century".

The landlady looked to be freshly bathed. The frills of her blouse and the iron-piled curls on her head seemed slightly aggressive, maybe because of the violent lighting behind the bar. I leant my back against photographically-reproduced plywood and studied her as she talked to her one customer.

"*You* ask him," she said, "he'll bloody clout me if I do."

The customer didn't seem to be doubting her; none the less she went on to prove that this was to be expected, by telling how her husband once beat her for wearing curling pins in her hair when she went to bed.

You would think that to tell such a story would humiliate her. But she wasn't humiliated, because the story glamorized her husband. It brought out his tough qualities that are particularly admired in a pub landlord. In other words, her humiliating story was good for trade in the pub; it was far from being humiliating, because everyone respects something that's done for the sake of trade.

I didn't expect this to be a place where I could stay for the night. Nevertheless, I asked.

"We stopped doing guests now, love," she said. "It isn't worth it. You won't find anywhere nearer than town."

I went out and stumbled through the stony fields.

I learnt, that evening, something that I would never, otherwise, have discovered about a place so near to my own home: I learnt how difficult it is, here, to find somewhere to stay for the night. It is,

I learnt, a place that doesn't expect visitors, either commercial ones or holiday-makers. "Who'd want to stay a night in Huddersfield?" one landlady asked me—expecting to find it easier in a big town, I had caught a bus into Huddersfield.

People were coming home from work. Amongst the dark-clothed inheritors of this town I saw that special brightness that I see in many of the Victorian and Edwardian streets of Oldham, Halifax, Huddersfield and Bradford, where the damp and the dry rot have driven many English people away: it was the brightness of the Pakistani and Indian communities, who come here clothed in brilliantly white or patterned textiles, and are eventually taught by the prolonged winters and by the insidious dirt that it is best to cover that native brightness with drab, impermanent English clothes. Huddersfield has one of the largest Pakistani communities in England; many of them were on the streets as I went from pub to pub, looking for somewhere to stay.

I began by taking a pint of beer before I asked the landlord or landlady if there was a room to spare. Then I cut to half pints. Eventually I did no more than ask for a room; beer drinking was taking up the whole of the night, and I was getting drunk. Each landlady sent me to her friend, but I seemed always to be without luck. It was a strange feeling to be within a few miles of my home, and yet to be homeless. I followed directions that turned out to be absurd, leading me stumbling in the dark through the mud and unset cement and windy unlit spaces of the vast roadworks that are ringing Huddersfield like a fortification. Near to its vast railway station, I stood embarrassed in my muddy shoes on the carpet of the grandest hotel in town. Luckless, I went away, directed for half a mile beyond the roadworks again, to a hotel kept by a polite Indian whose English was immaculate, like his clothes, and who was more helpful, and who telephoned hotels for me.

There was a room to be had in a pub called The Miller's Rest. I went back into town, following the Indian's directions, and got lost.

There was a man tottering in the street, and I asked him the way.

"Come with me, boss, I'll show you, I'm going there," he said. He began to tell me about the place through which we were walking; judging from his passion, this was the continuation of a conversation—or a monologue—which had been unwillingly broken. It was already fairly close to closing time in the pubs; but I wondered why he had left the pubs so early. Perhaps he was hurrying home to a fearful wife.

"This area was supposed to be a redevelopment area," he said. "It was supposed to be made better. And what have they done? They put swings and goodness knows what near to where old people are living and of course the teenagers are there until goodness knows what time so there's all sorts of goings-on and these old people have no peace at all. It isn't fair, is it, boss?"

I agreed.

"It was supposed to be made better, but it's just got worse and worse. All that money that's been put into it has been wasted because what they've done, they've let the Pakistanis in. If you don't know these Pakistanis and how they carry on I'll take you for a trot round here sometime and show you some of these houses and you'll wonder why anyone agrees that these people should be allowed into the country."

"I'd love to," I said, "but I'm——"

"I bought my house twelve or fourteen years ago and altered it no end of a lot; now, we're pestered wi' them sort. They allowed two people to sleep in every room including the bathroom. There are twelve to fourteen people living in the house next to mine. There's a house along there, I wouldn't keep nanny goats in. And nanny goats *are* damned dirty. These Pakistanis don't use toilets as we do. It's against their religion to sit on a toilet. Do you know what they do? They stand on the seat. Or, they wrap it up, in newspaper. Just in town there they have these concrete tubs and one thing and another for plants. The plants have all been tore out, and you'll find packets of excreta in them. Or you'll find it, maybe, behind a rainwater pipe, wrapped up in newspaper.

"I've worked in these mills and places and it's amazing what trouble the bosses have with them. An instance of one down Oldham. This was the foreman that were telling me this. He went to look round and the chap that were on this loom had made a right mess of it, so he went into the office to tell the manager. The boss said, 'It can't be. He's one of the best men we have working for us.' He said it must be a mistake; so finally they both went to have a look.

"Well, when his boss saw the chap that were at the loom, he said 'Who are you?! What are you doing here?'—he didn't recognize him. 'Where's so-and-so?' he asked.

"'Oh, he sell me the job,' this chap says. 'He go work somewhere else.'"

We were walking through dark streets. Suddenly there was a fierce noise, and a blast of hot air, and a glimpse of brilliantly lit machinery as we passed doors opened to a mill. Then the darkness of houses and closed little shops repeated itself.

"You going hiking or someat?" he asked, as if he had just noticed my rucksack.

"I'm having a few days off," I said.

He wasn't very interested in me. He went back to the Pakistanis.

"You go to the swimming baths here," he said, "it's like jumping in the bloody Ganges.

"Do you know they don't pay income tax for the first twelve months? If you start working here, *you* do—and you're bred and born here.

"Now you get married—you're a young Englishman. You find your own home. You furnish it. Out of your own pocket. Now these people—they find a house, they get £100 towards the furniture from the government. A lot of people won't believe that. But I know it's true.

"In one place, where they was still on coal for the boilers, the engineers wanted someone to help move a load that had been tipped. But it was against the religion of these Pakistanis to shovel coal. And they wouldn't shovel it.

"Anyway, they came down from the office. 'Are you going to move it?'

"'No. 'Gainst our religion to shovel coal.'

"'Righto,' said the boss, 'go on up. You can have your cards'—and they moved it.

"It isn't a case of your wanting to change their religion or any other thing for that matter; only their ways of living. You can never believe anything they tell you.

"I'm representative for my terrace on the Residents' Association, and I've been a time or two to this house with some forms that had to be filled up. But as soon as they see me, some of these people, they *will* not come to the door. So I says to the council officials, 'Send your own men and let them have a try.'

"This Council official went and because they didn't recognize him this woman opened the door. But when he told her what he'd come for, 'Me no understand,' she says, 'me no speak English.' So he came to me and told me.

"'I'll go with yer,' I says.

"'Why?' he says. 'Can you get them to give information?'

"I says, 'You know they're in, don't you? You go and knock and put your foot in the door and I'll be round the corner and whip in.'

"'Oh,' he says, 'we don't want to have any trouble.'

"'Look,' I says, 'the only way to get information out of these people is to force it out of them. And I'll get that information from them in English.'

"He says, 'How do you know?'

"I says, 'Because she's a teacher of English for the Pakistanis. That's how I know she can speak English.'

"There was one I was looking for: he was never at home when I went. I saw his brother. 'Now,' I says, 'I'm still looking for your brother. Where is he?' 'In London.' 'When's he coming back?' 'I don't know.' 'Well, when he comes back tell him I want to see him. I'm fed up going round and getting no answer, so as soon as he comes back tell him I want to see him.'

"Just then his brother walked round the corner.

"I've complained about all this but nobody will do anything about it; and that's why I get annoyed, because no action's being taken.

"They fetched the Housing Minister to open some new developments that had been done with grants. The corporation arranged that he would come and look at a lady up the road and at me; he was going to look at two houses that had been done with this redevelopment job. But that lady's and mine had been altered for years.

"The Planning Department told me that he'd arrived and that he'd be coming up here at about twenty past eleven. I waited. I wanted him to come because I should tell him straight out that this wasn't altered with the redevelopment. But he never came. I got a letter from the council apologizing that he hadn't time, they were very sorry, But I know why—it was because somebody had told him that I was going to have a go at him.

"Everybody's frightened of having racial prejudice thrown at them. Some of us met five of the Race Relations Board at the Town Hall. They were there for us to put our complaints and questions to; and of course we were there for them to put their views to us.

"Anyway, this police superintendent wanted us to put our questions to him regarding the police, etc., first, as he'd another meeting to go to later on.

"Well, I started to question him. When he answered me I said, 'Excuse me, but there's one question I want to ask you. You know we know this area that we represent; now,' I said, 'do *you* know it?' 'Oh,' he says, 'I've heard of the new development area.' I says, 'I'm not wanting to know if you've *heard* of it. I want to know if you *know* it.' I says, 'Can you take me round this area as well as I can take you? You're a policeman, you should do.'

"He didn't know where it was! He's on the Race Relations Board, he should know what he's talking about when he comes to meet us. Now out of the five, three of them had never been to this area. Why do we go and talk to these people? We're wasting time. You think they'd come up here and have a look."

The man slowed down. He was standing outside a door in a dark terraced street; it seemed that he wanted me to leave before he went inside.

"It's been a problem and it's getting worse. I warned them what would happen. It's what's happened in America. Town's is going to be taken over."

For the first time, he stared at me, without having anything to say, his deep fund of prejudice spent. He was smiling.

"Is this where The Miller's Rest is?" I asked him.

He laughed. "You know that place where I met you? You was standing right by it then!"

"But what did you bring me here for?"

"I just wanted your company for a while." He opened the door. "Goodnight, boss."

I made my way back to The Miller's Rest, as well as I remembered it. All round me the lengthy ceremonies of parting, drunkenly, were being acted outside pub doors.

"Goodnight! Goodnight! Tarra!"

"Neet, then. Tarra!"

"Goodnight!"

Voices faded out of sound. It was after closing time in the pubs, but the door was unlocked when I strode over the sick spilled on to the steps of The Miller's Rest and entered a huge-roomed, brown and cream place, where the departed tide of customers had left a floor silted with cigarette butts and spilled beer, and the landlady was emptying the cigarette trays off the tables, on to these floor spillings.

"Were you the one that phoned for a room? I was just going to lock up." I took the room without inspecting it.

11

THE NEXT MORNING I caught a bus to Elland, and walked the same road past Mr Nicholls' mill. The last building on the road was a farm ringed by abandoned vehicles; then, through a gap in the walls where a dog kennelled in a barrel kept the sheep from straying off the moor and down the road, the road straightened through un-walled moorland. The sun was shining; but even so, to turn on to the moor's blow of silence and cold was like being pole-axed. The cold seemed to be reaching, relentlessly, for my bones. The moor was raked by clawed shadows of the clouds blown rapidly across the sun; travelling strings of light broke into the shifting brilliances of the red and gold of whinberry and bracken. There were also white acres of dried, sapless grass stalks. As the wind stirred the sunlit tops of these through their shadows, and as they were crossed by the shadows of clouds, the patches of grass seemed to etherealize; they seemed to become patches of pale, drifting vapour. But because of the cold that made my eyes ache if I opened them widely, it was difficult to do more than take an odd glance under the wind at the landscape. Somewhere, at a distance impossible to measure, a scrap of polythene glittered. More stable, near the roadside, an armchair rotted into the gold and brown of the bog. There was no one else walking this road. After a few miles it joined a main road at a place where cars stop on gravel on top of bare rock overlooking Marsden Moor.

Here, alone, I was engulfed by the space over the sudden drop; it seemed to be entirely sky. Below me was one reservoir. Far off— how far?—a glittering bar in what seemed to be sky was another reservoir, that caught the sun on a distant moor, the soft greys of which sank into the haze of the sky. A line of poles from a dis-continued telephone line led to a deserted hotel, built rather grandly to "command the view". Beyond a spur of moor, at the end of the valley, the mills clutter into the black smudge of Marsden; in Marsden is a mill which is still partly surrounded by a stone barricade, with loopholes for cannon, built to defend the mill against the attacks of the Luddites in 1812.

In that year, two Marsden blacksmiths, Enoch and James Taylor, began making "cropping frames", intending to supply them to local mills. The cropping frame was a pair of hand-cropping shears clamped to a frame and controlled by a wheel to travel over the length of a piece of cloth, clipping the woolly "nap" off the cloth as it moved. It was a clumsy and inoffensive device; but it was worked by only one man, and it could do the work of ten hand-croppers.

In the same year, Napoleon's continuing blockade of foreign ports; the war with the United States; and the bad harvests of 1810 and 1811 had made trade difficult, and the cost of living high. The cropping frame could save the cloth manufacturer from bankruptcy; so many were determined to use the frames, no matter what the opposition. There is a mill in Clitheroe, Lancashire, that was made like a medieval fortress, with a moat around it filled with water from the mill-lodge (reservoir) to defend it from the workers; in 1812, three men and a boy of fourteen were executed at Westhoughton, Lancashire, for burning down a cotton mill; and, despite such penalties, in 1826 a mob had destroyed almost every loom in Blackburn, Accrington and Darwen. William Horsfall of Marsden said that he was going to install cropping frames "even if I have to ride through blood to my saddle-girths to do it".[1] His threat was tested. The croppers, threatened with unemployment and starvation, determined on smashing the frames.

The first group of workers to smash cropping frames was led by Ned Ludd, in Nottingham; so when the movement spread through West Yorkshire, the groups were called Luddites. At that time every district of West Yorkshire had a group of Luddites, each led by a "general" or a "King Ludd". The King Ludd of the Colne Valley was George Mellor, a cropper who worked in his

---

[1] See *Colne Valley Cloth* by Phyllis Bentley, pub. The Huddersfield and District Woollen Export Group, 1947.

stepfather's cloth-dressing shop at Longroyd Bridge, near Hudders-field. The Luddites—Mellor and two friends from the same shop, Benjamin Walker and Thomas Smith; William Thorpe from a nearby shop; and thirty or forty others—made a vow of fraternity that they called "being twissed in"; meaning that they were now twisted into one body, as wool fibres are twisted into one thread.

They threatened mill-owners who used cropping frames; and they waged guerilla warfare, turning their knowledge of the Mars-den moors to their advantage against the strange soldiers who were sent to arrest them. They plotted their campaigns at isolated pubs, and they dispersed across the moors when they heard the jangling harness of the redcoats' horses. They blackened their faces and raided isolated farmhouses to steal fire-arms; and they drilled amongst the rocks and heather.

With "Old Enoch"—the name which they gave to a heavy hammer, named after Enoch Taylor so that they could use, as a rally cry, "Enoch makes them and Enoch breaks them"—they smashed a load of cropping frames being delivered across Liversedge Moor. They broke into mills at night to smash frames; and at one mill where they were surprised by the redcoats who defended it, two Luddites were killed. As a reprisal for this, George Mellor organized the murder of William Horsfall as he was crossing Crosland Moor on market day, 28 April 1812.

Though most people in the Colne Valley knew who the murderers were, their secret was kept, despite a £2,000 reward, until the autumn, when the Luddites were betrayed by one of their own members, Benjamin Walker. The movement then lost its vigour. Other Luddites became "untwissed", as breaking the oath was called. Wholesale trials of the Luddites took place in York in January 1813. Many croppers were transported and the murderers, with the ex-ception of Walker, were hanged—Walker, when released from prison, returned and lived to an old age in the Colne Valley, despised by his neighbours.

The Luddites were the first, I think, to protest, to the point of sacrificing their own lives, against the machine. They were naïve, not realizing that without being part of a national revolution they were bound to be hunted down as criminals; but they were brave, they kicked against misery, and they represented the vigour that has given way to West Yorkshire apathy displayed, for instance, in the shameful lack of a memorial to them in Marsden or on its moors. Maybe that abandoned, depressing and starkly-obvious hotel building could be turned into their museum.

The Pennine Way cuts across the moors here, crossing the hilltops above the Saddleworth Valley. But this is one of the less well-defined sections; to reach Saddleworth, I lost the footpath and floundered across the moor.

Usually the easiest way over the moorland is to follow the stream to a watershed, then leap the runnels through the peat bog until you find a stream running downhill on the other side. Leaping from stone to stone over the red water needs as much alacrity as does crossing from tussock to tussock of grass on the open moor; but by the stream you can, at least, see where you are putting your feet—on the moor you are never sure how far your feet are going to sink between the grass clumps, and may fear at every step to jolt your spine or sink into hidden water.

Climbing the streams, crossing patches of high moor, I was making towards the Castleshaw Valley, where there was once a Roman fort. I met a man with a dog. He was not wearing those excessively practical clothes, every inch zipped or hooked against the wind, that hikers wear; nor were his shoes and donkey jacket impractical for the moors; nor did he wear the tattered coat and trousers of some scrounger from the towns. He was, unmistakably, a farmer, with a casual command of the place in which we met.

Without undue interest, he stared at my coming. Then, despite our being the only people on that great open moor, both man and dog decided that I was without interest to them. As we met, the dog panted on a dry stone, and stared balefully at me; and, before I could say "Hullo", the man turned to the wall and peed.

I took that to be a discouragement to conversation, and passed him by. It was oddly disconcerting.

As I dropped downhill towards Saddleworth there were little patches of slatey coal on which nothing whatsoever grows; they were the remains of abortive nineteenth-century excavations for coal.

———————

12

SADDLEWORTH IS A thin projection of Yorkshire down a long, winding valley into Lancashire and Cheshire.

The map makes it seem obvious that it should belong to either Lancashire or Cheshire; and administratively, it seems it should belong to one or the other—it is served by Lancashire schools, hospitals and shops; and its people mostly commute into Lancashire or Cheshire for their work.

But Saddleworth, for a long while, clung tenaciously to its status as a Yorkshire place. Traditionally, its woollen industry belongs to Yorkshire, separating it from the surrounding cotton towns. So the original Saddleworth people, the few of them who are left, feel that they would lose something by "going in with Oldham". More precise about their feelings, the people who have come to live here don't want anyone else to live in Saddleworth; so the "campaign to keep Saddleworth Yorkshire", when it was waged whilst I lived there about ten years ago, drew most of its strength from these new people, who knew that to be united with Oldham or Ashton-under-Lyne, the neighbouring Lancashire towns, might mean overspill towns. Like a small old state weak in arms, Saddleworth tried to support its independence by making much of its "character" and its particular "culture".

Saddleworth is, today, the generic name for a group of villages whose names—Dob Cross, Denshaw, Diggle, and Delph—when pronounced together make a musical phrase with a heavy, mechanical rhythm, like a brass-band tune insensitively played; or like a line of verse by Saddleworth's deceased poet, Ammon Wrigley:

It's good to be in Saddleworth in the spring time of the year . . .

(who did, however, balance his mechanical, didactic and sentimental verse with other books recounting his life here in natural, attractive prose).

Until the motor car made it accessible from surrounding towns, and houses that hadn't quite disappeared quickly became valuable, Saddleworth, for the whole of this century, had been steadily collapsing into grassed-over ruins amongst the stones natural to the place. The higher up the hillsides the houses were, the earlier they were abandoned; hence that destroyed and naked look of its uplands.

The original Saddleworth—a hamlet built on the hill when the sites of those other, later villages to which it has given its name were no more than intractable marshes—hardly exists any more. It has been thinned to a scattering of "converted" cottages. On the site of a succession of churches since Norman times, it has a Victorian church as stark and black as a mill building; and there remain two pubs, the Church Inn and The Cross Keys, which the motor car saved, just in time, so that they might become typical of most contemporary English pubs in every county. If you follow the footpath by the stream downhill from the church, to a place where the cattle don't stray and which is uncultivated because of the stones, you might stumble through tall and tangled weeds on to the foundations of the original village.

I lived in Saddleworth for eight years—first of all in Delph; then in a cottage called Primrose Cottage on a hill called Primrose Hill. The primroses were a casualty of social mobility after the second world war; they were dug up and transported to gardens, and for twenty years no one had seen a primrose there but of course, in the memories of older people at any rate, they once flourished there.

Primrose Hill is now covered by a hair of that sickly grass that reddens many hillsides when it dies in the autumn. It is bumpy with stones fallen from houses and walls; grey sheep, that look like stones until they stir, wander over it like the ghosts of lost tribes.

Still higher, above what was once cultivated land, is a cliff of black, gritty rocks, sparkling a little with silver silica, and swept by rains into anthropomorphic shapes. The rains have worn little bowls out of the tops of some of these stones, and the bowls retain water. According to local folklore, the water in these bowls is a magical cure for blindness and for diseases of the eye.

Beyond the cliff is a plateau, cut by a maze of ditches washed naturally out of the peat, and divided by one long, deep, wide ditch that is an abortive nineteenth-century drain. Looking one direction across that space, with occasional distant headlands rising to mix with the misty air, their hard rocks sometimes seeming more soft than the clouds, one gets a sense of immeasurable loneliness; in the other direction, one overlooks Lancashire, which is like a dark, level sea, where one can see, sometimes, buildings like the CWS building in the centre of Manchester. On the plateau, in midsummer, cotton grass blooms, in sparse white spots over the drier ground, in thick white clusters where it flourishes in the marshy places. In this generally grimy landscape, the new clean white of the cotton-grass heads is startlingly beautiful; I used to gather it and put it in vases in our cottage.

I remember Saddleworth as a place where, at certain moments, a generally dull landscape broke for short periods into vivid life. Spring was always a disappointment; I always missed the mighty surge of growth of other places. It was always late, and always brief. But late summer, when the cotton grass bloomed in the bogs, was beautiful because of it; and autumn was unique, when a mist tinted purple by the heather made the hills mysterious; and underfoot and over the banks was a dressing of the brilliant purple of heather, of the yellow of gorse, and of the sonorous darkness of the darkening herbage.

It was most exciting when it snowed; exciting because of the beauty of it, and also because of the vitality it suddenly drew from people.

There rarely fell more than a few inches of snow. Our trouble, and our excitement, came when the wind followed the snow and blew, as it often did, for several days, maybe for a week or more. The wind lifted the snow into the air, and kept it there, boiling, in a constant blinding fury, and it felt as though this constant fury and noise and blindness would drive you mad if it would not give up.

The back of the house faced the direction from which the wind whipped the snow off the moors, banking it against our wall, and leaving the high rocks bare black streaks above the snow fields. The snow blew into the house through crannies: and we couldn't open the door to shovel the piling snow out, because of the wind. The door, and the window of the lean-to kitchen there, we lined with rags and towels, which quickly became saturated in the creeping snow, and later froze in their war against the draughts. We used the front door, which was usually more sheltered, for me to go out as infrequently as possible, maybe once a day, to the coal that was stored in the neighbouring barn. Between the door of the house and the door of the barn—maybe fifteen yards—it was possible to be lost. I remember pausing in doubt, and staring into the whirls of snow in an attempt to see patterns in the movement, until the frantic patterns made me dizzy. On these trips out for coal, I remember, the warmth of my face melted the snow that fell upon it, so I returned, after only a few moments, numbed and dripping with icicles. We were not a family that anticipated crises; so we moved with increasing fearfulness to the last tins of food. We sat close to the fire, continuously shifting the side of our bodies burned by the fire and warming the side that was becoming numb with cold from the draught; and we hoped that the snow would not bring down the electricity pylons. If the room at night suddenly darkened, we would take a candle to warm a hole in the florid patterns of frost on the window, to see if the neighbouring houses were also dark.

And then, when the wind at last ceased, a pristine whiteness— as when the cotton grass bloomed—covered the landscape; and even, where the snow drifted, gave the landscape new shapes; and a new silence came over it, the sounds of movement were muffled in the snow, and the main roads over the hills were blocked, except to the snow-ploughs which we watched, on the far hills, day and night. When they could move without the wind hindering them, their flashing lights turned strangely, reflected on the whiteness.

When the snow stopped blowing, it was a signal for everyone

to leave their houses and struggle through the drifts by whatever route they could find down to the village to buy food. At one moment, I would go out into this new stillness, and see the people, about whom I'd known nothing for a week, leaving their doors at the same time; and I could calculate where, lower down—usually on the road, as far up it as the snow plough had reached—we were all going to meet and go into the village in a pack.

Whilst I lived in that cottage, I taught art to some of my neighbours in the local Further Education Institute, and also to some of their children in the local Secondary School; and I then first gave myself several days a week in which to write. I wrote poems, and little else. I made that poetry out of a few simple elements; for what else did I have? There were the changes in weather over a landscape of rushes, heather and half-secret outbursts of water, with its wandering sheep and its broken farms, its sparseness combated by a richer growth that had been in my imagination since childhood; there was the industrial and suburban life of the valleys; there were aspects of marital and family life, known in my own experience and partly seen in the lives of others. So I wrote poems about the smoke rising from the chimney of a distant farm; about the sparse life of a huddle of houses called a "village"; about the sheep; about the twilights, the snow, and walking on the cold bareness of the moor in winter; about absence and longing; and about the few birds that inhabited the moor, the curlews, and the little flocks of twittering finches.

Preparatory to poems, I spent long hours of the day in walks alone, or in sitting on the cottage step, watching the vast drama of sky and moor.

I had never in my life before spent long periods, day after day through several years and through all the changes of seasons, contemplating the changes over the same landscape. From this cottage door, level with the tops of the hills so that they seemed like the crests of waves disappearing northwards towards Northumberland and Scotland, this most solid of landscapes, made of bare rocks and treeless slopes and black mill towns, seemed a constantly mobile, liquid one, as it was transformed by the weather. In one valley it might be raining; in another the sun might be shining; and I could watch these weathers moving, and guess which was approaching. The moving clouds often seemed more solid than the hills they veiled. I learnt there how varied mists, that constant element in which we lived, could be. There were mists that seemed as delicate as grey flower petals strewn on the valley floor. These were so transparent, their edges were so faint and constantly, subtly changing, you could tell that they were there only by contrast to certain brutally outlined rocks and headlands that stood above them. There were more solid mists that hid the valleys, rocking in the valleys like porridge in a bowl, but throwing tongues of mist into the air, and up the sides of the hills. There were mists that gathered at the ends of valleys and pushed black fists over the tops of hills and gradually widened until they engulfed us in a storm of hail or snow.

I watched that landscape almost as much during the night as I did during the day.

One summer night, when I was concentrating on a poem, I was startled by a noise outside. The most familiar noise can be frightening if your mind is not prepared to accept it; if, for instance, a friend taps you on the shoulder when you did not hear his approach. This was the noise of stones falling off a wall—something that happens at the slightest disturbance in this landscape laced with old drystone walls.

I went to the door. A full moon had risen over an utterly clear landscape, the blue hills running like a frozen sea; and a flock of sheep, attracted by my light, had gathered round the cottage.

As they stood in a semi-circle their eyes shone jade-green in the light. The sheep, too, seemed petrified. This look of petrifaction made the moment magical, as if it were outside time, a few moments that did not exist as time, because they were without change.

Then suddenly the spell was broken, one of the sheep panicked away, and the others followed. They clattered up the hillside.

That night, and through the next morning, I wrote the poem "Beasts":

> At night, surrounding the house,
> their fear impregnates summer air
> as muffled and crazy as moths
> they stumble amongst the gorse.
>
> What's that? What's that?
> Laying poems aside, I go to see.
> They stare: as if my stare
> stunned them. Then race,
>
> fleece combed in gorse and wire
> towards a moorline stark as cold black iron
> in the twilit midnight, under the moon. . . .

My landlord, who was also my only neighbour for some distance, must have thought, as he saw me sitting on the steps of my cottage for so long and so frequently, that I spent most of my time taking breaks from writing. Sometimes he seemed a little offended and irritated by this; for he had to go to work. But he was, as they say, a little bit "yonderly" himself—meaning, for ever looking yonder, that is into the distance, dreamily, so that he stumbled over what was immediately present. Sometimes he praised my everlasting, ever-surprising good fortune, as it seemed to him: "If you fell off the Co-Op cart you'd land in the dividend," he said. He was an amateur artist. Like nearly all the members of the local art group, he used to paint hill landscapes, which he saw—which all the art group saw—as a drab, military grey. He drew the patterns of stone walls lacing the moors, the mill towns at the foot, and maybe a patterning of comic and caricatured figures, that was supposed, I think, to derive from L. S. Lowry. Only he, underneath, was a little more flamboyant. Whether he expressed it or not, I don't know; but I suspected that he'd rather like to make a gesture like Gauguin's; to throw off his job as a clerk, and even if he was perhaps too timid to go off to the tropics (or maybe it wouldn't appeal to him), perhaps to stay at home, as I did, and live off whatever came his way, as I did, and paint hill landscapes. He liked to come smoking his pipe and tell me art-group gossip: who had been there to "give them a talk" and so on. But he didn't have much time for this—or even for painting. I only recognized that he *was* a painter because of a few prematurely aged oil paintings about the place; their oil had sunk into the hardboard, leaving patches of dull, and patches of glossy oil. He spent most of his time, whilst I was there, labouring to level a lawn and a garden out of a stony slope of a kind that gardeners in level country have often painfully imitated with built rockeries and with those plants, like heather, that are difficult to grow in fertile places, but were natural to Primrose Hill. My neighbour, on the other hand, struggled to stock his garden with the plants that could barely survive on an exposed and rocky hillside— what the snow or the frost or the wind did not destroy, the sheep did, determinedly breaking or jumping walls and fences because of the lack of succulent food outside the garden. I learnt there that there was hardly any garden plant other than foxgloves that these sheep, at any rate, couldn't eat; consequently, foxgloves grew fairly well there.

Both he and his wife were frenetically busy about their house and garden—at any rate, they were busy with the garden, and with keeping the house's sober antiques glowing with polish. The roof of their house, and the roof of my cottage, had deep sags in them, signifying rotten and about-to-collapse timbers. Houses here always collapsed the same way: the roofs gave in first, usually suddenly and "unexpectedly". It happened often. The only house that was higher up the moors than ours, and which was empty, fell one winter's night.

On another night, in a high wind, the roof of the little barn that connected my house with the house of my neighbour fell into the lane, bringing a few feet from the top of the wall with it.

The noise, heard from inside my bedroom, was cataclysmic, terrifying. I went out and met my neighbours inspecting it in the wind and the dark. Then we went back to bed. The next day, they tidied some of the stones from where they had fallen. They talked of making the new space into a "walled garden", and went back to tending unsuccessful azaleas, rhododendrons, and tulips, continuing to ignore our comically sagging roofs. He went around with a little hammer, tapping the stones; or he dug with pick and spade, and climbed ladders; she, perpetually in that haste often adopted as a habit by hill dwellers because of their need to guard themselves against the cold, scurried past me on her errands to the village.

I read Erich Fromm's *The Fear Of Freedom* whilst I was there; and I thought that maybe this absurdity of a garden, which I never saw them sit down in, look at, and enjoy contemplatively—only I did that—this restless energy that they expended on repetitive tasks, was an instinctive means for them to save themselves from the loneliness of a freedom, where there'd be no demanding tasks, but only the time-space in which to choose and to think.

As she rushed past my door, she would throw out questions about my "work". Her questions were partly polite, and partly pragmatic: she wanted assurance that I could pay the rent. I would answer briefly, not only because I found it boring to tell her what I was doing, but also because, like the White Rabbit in *Alice in Wonderland*, she hardly had time to wait for an answer. When she didn't quite catch my mumbled replies, she would cut me short with one of her catch-phrases: "You're working for posterity, not for prosperity" she would suggest to me. But I was grateful for her sympathy for my vocation, for I was forced to pay our rent irregularly.

Saddleworth has in its vernacular two terms to describe its new-comers. There are "foreigners", that is those who were born here, but whose ancestors settled within the period of someone's knowing;

and "comers-in", who are those who in their own life-times had settled here.

My neighbours represented the gentility of the comers-in. They came thirty years ago, when, like all true pioneers and frontier families, they fought a battle against the natives—who not only, as a majority, spurned them a little; they were actively malicious.

In primitive hill communities like this one, he who can, by legal right or brute force, control the water supply, has a major control over life; and one trick was to turn the spring water supply into the fields, so that it did not reach the house.

Cows were collected in the lanes; and their droppings were left to form a quagmire.

But by the time I came, the comers-in were dominant.

For them, the pubs demolished their interior walls and encrusted the new spaces with polystyrene fakes; and the newsagents stocked *Vogue* and *She* and the *Observer* and the *Sunday Times*.

For them, the premises of little old parish industries were converted to sauna baths and art galleries; the old shops in the High Street changed hands cheaply and brightened into valuable boutiques, restaurants, Do-It-Yourself shops, and estate offices.

Because of them, the quarry that had been slowly, over a century, unveiling the view of Oldham that lay beyond the hill, found itself "pilloried", as they say, in the local press.

They organized regular art festivals; and for them, the rough corners of the villages were formalized with municipal floral displays.

Their almost-fashionable women seemed idle in their homes and in the streets during the day; they looked available, although they weren't; some of them went into pubs, alone; and for many of them the Further Education Institute flourished excessively, with classes in cake-decorating, flower-arranging, dog-training, pottery, holiday-makers' Spanish, art, and my own creative writing.

In fact, these were the ones who sympathized with me when I surfaced, always bearded, always caricatured as an eccentric, in the newspapers: "If you see a bearded man declaiming verse on

Saddleworth Moor at daybreak, or in the village graveyard or outside an Oldham mill, just pretend you haven't noticed"; and "leaning over tombstones, drinking in a pub, bathing in the zinc tub that passes for a bath in his moorland cottage—that is how ideas come to poet Glyn Hughes".

But the "originals", like the rooted natives of most places, were less approachable.

Very few of them, I think, had been the ones to make big profits out of property, though some of them did realize, just in time, what was happening; and quite a few of those, vaguely calculating, refused to sell their barns and cottages and subsidiary farmhouses, allowing them instead to collapse a little more each winter.

Inarticulate; educated to fear such places as doctors' surgeries, headmasters' waiting rooms, lawyers' offices, and to cover that fear with bravado; not knowing what "environment" and "comprehensive education" and "élitism" were; not learning the modern techniques of "protest" from the newspapers that *they* read; not having learnt to form groups the modern way, through coffee mornings, women's lib., Tupper-ware parties, and meetings after the keep-fit class, they were largely unable to affect public decisions.

The men went into the factories, mostly in Oldham and the other nearby towns, early in the mornings, and returned home inept for anything but the most somnambulant social life—watching television or, at best, desultory conversations in the pubs. Their women were similarly hidden away in the mills; or they carried buckets around the farms. They were never amongst the decision-makers behind social events; they were always the lackeys, who brewed tea and buttered bread.

The past generations of this valley once had great vigour. They took a most militant part in social change. Delph, one of the Saddleworth villages, is known as a place that would not accept defeat after the Peterloo Massacre; the people continued to prepare for revolution, with caches of scythes and sharpened sickles hidden in barns and mill-lofts. It was a lady from Saddleworth, Annie Kenney, who with Christabel Pankhurst, began the Suffragette Movement by protesting for votes for women at a Manchester election meeting in 1905.

In this place, as in all other places nearby, the same urge that made Lancashire and Yorkshire people so extraordinarily inventive and enterprising industrially, made them also determined on improving themselves through education. William Holt is a living example of that determined effort to become educated; and as E. P. Thompson wrote in *The Making of the English Working Class*,

Every district had its weaver-poets, biologists, mathematicians, musicians, geologists, botanists . . . There are northern museums and natural history societies which still possess records or collections of lepidoptera built by the weavers; whilst there are accounts of weavers in isolated villages who taught themselves geometry by chalking on their flagstones, and who were eager to discuss the differential calculus.

The shelves of local history books in all small town libraries in Lancashire and in Yorkshire show the enormous will to participate in culture, to produce belles-lettres. Each valley has its still-revered poet; Tim Bobbin, and Sam Bamford, and Saddleworth's Ammon Wrigley. It was a Saddleworth weaver, John o' Grinfilt (John of Greenfield) who wrote a poem of chilling, terrible pathos:

Awm a poor cotton weaver, as mony a one knows,
Aw've nowt t'ate in the house, and aw've wore
    out me clothes,
You'd hardly give sixpence for all aw've got on,
Me clogs are worn out, an' stockings aw've none;
You'd think it were hard, to be sent into th'world
To clem and do best as you can.

Our parish-church parson kept telling us long,
We'd see better times if we'd but 'old our tongue;
Aw've holden my tongue, til aw can hardly
    draw breath,

Aw think in me heart he means to clem me to death;
Aw know he lives well, with back-biting the Devil,
But he never picked o'er in his life.

We held on six weeks, thinking each day were
　　the last,
We tarried and shifted, til now we're quite fast;
We've lived upon nettles, whilst nettles were good,
And Waterloo porridge were the best of our food;
Awm telling you true, aw can find folk enough
That are living no better than me.

Our Margaret declares, if who'd clothes to put on,
Who'd go up to London to see the great man;
An' if things didn't alter, when there who had bin,
Who says who'd begin and fight blood up to th'e'en,
Who's nought against King, but who likes a fair
　　thing,
And who says who can tell when who's hurt.

That culture was remembered and revered well enough. John o' Grinfilt's poem, which was sung as a ballad at the time of the Napoleonic Wars, was sung in Saddleworth pubs—and not only by young folk singers who had heard it sung by A. L. Lloyd on a Topic record, but also by old people, ignorant of Folk Singing Clubs, to whom it had been passed orally through generations, and who sang it to you as a privilege, feeling themselves to be representing a tradition that ought not to be given away lightly.

Experience has made me bashful about calling myself a poet when I'm in a pub; but here, older people looked at me in a friendly, respectful way if I was introduced as a "poet"; and they would quote Ammon Wrigley's verse at me, embarrassing me because I wouldn't dare to quote my own verse back at them. There was an Ammon Wrigley Society that held hot-pot suppers in the Church Inn; the landlord of the Church Inn was able to recite verse after verse of Ammon Wrigley poems.

But to remember a tradition is not enough. Now, if these people were to survive, they had to enter another culture.

And they couldn't do it. They wouldn't do it. That new culture was about them, but they couldn't get into it; it mocked them, with its glitter.

I always saw Saddleworth as a place of conflicts; of violent conflicts that were, perhaps, as much products of that violent weather over the denuded uplands, as they were a products of social forces. And these conflicts were expressed, from time to time, in murders.

Around the church is a tangled graveyard, with monuments which are much older than the church. Visitors most often go to the grave of two men who were murdered in the "Bills o' Jacks murder". At the end of the nineteenth century, two men, a father and his son, were cut to pieces with an axe in an isolated pub which they kept on the moors off the road from Greenfield to Holmfirth. The murder, a famous newspaper story of the time, was never solved. Various people were accused. The most colourful of the accused were the "platters": these were part-gypsy, part-tramp people who lived in makeshift shelters on the moors, and earned a living by weaving rush baskets. The platters claimed rights to rush patches on the moors, and it was thought that they murdered the innkeeper and his son in a quarrel over their rush-cutting rights.

And almost everyone in England knows about the notorious "Moors Murders", in which Brady and Hindley buried the bodies of children on that moor at the back of the house in which we lived.

And it almost seemed, to me, that it was a significant symptom of the place, that there should be gloating over the "Bills o' Jacks murder"; and that the series of, perhaps, the most sickening murders in our history, should be associated with Saddleworth.

Conflict seemed to be a continuous, defining feature of its life. It was a knowledge that their culture, slight though it was, had been fought for in the most bitter conflicts, that made the old people guard their inheritance; conflict with the weather, with the steep gradients, with the shallow soil, seemed to be an element of daily life; and almost, one might say that cheerfulness was a victory gained in conflict with colourless surroundings where few flowers grew.

So it seemed natural for me to think, whilst I lived in Saddleworth, that what interested me in art was the way in which it could feed and maintain endurance. To articulate experience, to construct lines of poetry, seemed to be a matter of refining the understanding so that it was not blunted by experience and could continue to be a useful exploratory tool. In the art of the past, I was excited by the theme of the fight to survive and to grow in opposition to the things that one is encouraged, or compelled, to think; and what moved me was the pathos and the loneliness intrinsic to that endurance. What I looked for and admired in people who were not artists was the ways that they found, other than by art, to maintain their endurance— the endurance of the individual's preferences, instincts, and prejudices; and also the endurance of the individual's sense of rightness, which might be deeply buried, and difficult to quarry, but which produces that stubborn resistance to the cogencies passed through society.

13

THE STREAM THAT trickles out of the soaked Saddleworth peat, and down the crannies in the rock that it washes so that they gleam, just there, in a tiny diamond or two of their native gold, is called the River Tame.

It quickly gathers enough grey, soupy water to be worth calling a river. Its valley broadens to contain the same mess of industrial towns as are found, for instance, along the River Calder. The River Tame flows through Mossley, Stalybridge, Dukinfield, Hyde and Stockport; then out of the country of which I write, to join the other rivers that make up the River Mersey. Within a loop of the small towns, it contains the great commercial city of Manchester.

All those towns are cotton towns. All except Manchester have a lot in common—Manchester being different because it is where the cotton was traded, and not woven; so it has huge commercial buildings, like its Cotton Exchange.

Northwards, continuing the loop made by the river, is another chain of towns: Middleton, Rochdale, and Oldham—whose districts have names that sound like the names of diseases: "Mumps" and "Grotton"; and which sound particularly appropriate for this dark mass that, from the millstone-grit cliffs overlooking it, seems to have flowed out of the hills.

The whole landscape is a basin, that was filled, extraordinarily rapidly, at the end of the eighteenth and the first part of the nineteenth centuries, by Irish immigrants, by demobilized soldiers, by agricultural workers, come to learn to weave.

On the edges of its housing estates, working-class towns, and industrial valleys, there are often half-heartedly cultivated areas where dwindling woodland and the dry, sooty stalks of grass unmown and ungrazed for many years covers the rapes, muggings, homosexual meetings, child-molesting, adulteries, and all other loves too secret to be consummated in rooms that have watchful neighbours.

This human life replaces wild life. Marauding gangs of town lads ("gorbies") intent on killing off the last relics of wild life in these places, scour the land, shooting every living thing apart from humans (and sometimes catching them, too); smashing fences, trees, birds' nests, outbuildings of farms, and bridges; and leaving uncollected beer bottles, contraceptives, and copies of the *Daily Mirror*, the *News Of the World*, and straight porn.

It is the natural life of the housing estate lad: I, who was one, know.

I do not remember what impulse herded us boys into a small gang, thrilled at carving a way through a head-high field of corn, smashing the windows in empty houses, breaking a hole in an orchard fence to steal fruit, smashing bridges over streams so that no one but us could follow the footpaths; only that it is, in my mind, mixed with the thrills of watching Flash Gordon and John Wayne in the cinema on Saturday afternoons, where their regardless attitude to baddies or to Indians was the same as ours to the proprietors of the countryside. The lives of its owners were so outside our experience, that we could not have any feeling for it, to counterbalance our lust and our adventure.

When harvesting the cornfields, in more genial counties such as the one where my childhood was spent, farmers cut a track around the perimeter of the field, and gradually approach the centre. In doing this, they drive the "vermin" to the last remaining square yards of cover. Then men and boys, as many as can be found, come to the field and stand around the edges with guns; or with sticks if they don't have guns. Only then are the last few yards of corn cut, compelling the rabbits and hares to dash across the stubble, and be easily slaughtered.

Intake Farm (so called because it was a piece of farmland bitten out of the moor for cultivation), where once Tommy Toat sheltered his life whilst another world circled around it, growing closer and closer, intent on destroying it, was like such an oasis of standing corn; within the tightening grip of the towns he preserved what he aggressively (though without articulating his thoughts) believed to be a good life.

Now Intake Farm is a stone skull with "Fuck" scrawled on its walls. The nettle bed that grows within and without the farmhouse smells of urine, which almost overcomes the usual pungency of nettle beds. You would hardly guess that the marshy patch of brighter grass at the side of the lane was once a spring, and the focus of life here. Tins and bottles have been thrown through where the windows and doors used to be.

Tommy Toat was a tiny, witty and intelligent man who could barely read and write—in childhood either snow or the demands of harvest-time had kept him from school. But he seemed to lack nothing in not being able to read or write; he seemed to lack nothing in never going away from Intake Farm—he never took a holiday, and called seaside towns "a good advertisement for concrete".

I knew him well, because for five years of my life I rented from him the labourer's cottage that was at the end of his building, with a small shippen separating it from his house.

That low grey building was half sunk into the earth, as if it had grown within a wave of those grasslands, rather than to have been erected upon them. The roof rose from the house and over the barn and swept down on the other side; gabled extensions bulged out of it, with mullioned windows that had slipped to a tilt with the one-sided sinking of the earth beneath; and all its bulging extensions seemed to have grown organically, rather than to have been planned.

I imagined that, at different moments in its 400-years' history, someone with nothing to do on a summer's day had gone out and built a bit more to his house wherever, at that moment, his fancy prompted him to build. No plans; the house rose into its shapes, during the summer days, as flour rises to the shapes of a loaf in the oven.

At that time, I earned a meagre living by gardening at suburban houses; and also, having recently left art school, by using my teacher training to teach rural studies at a school in a nearby mess of streets and factories called Flowery Field.

At Flowery Field, as in all northern towns, a maze of fencing made of industrial detritus confined those bizarre collections of greenhouses, hen-pens, immaculately cultivated flower and vegetable plots clinging to scraps of ground left over from building, and called "allotments". They have always seemed, to me, to demonstrate how new, how little rooted, industrialization still is; the rural life that was left only a few generations ago exerts itself so persistently in the lives of the descendants of those who were herded from the country into the industrial towns. These allotments were cultivated by the parents and the grandparents of the lads I taught rural studies to, who themselves were the ones who had that irresistible impulse to track through the countryside with guns and dogs; so, I imagined, a basic interest in my subject was there, in Flowery Field.

The soil of the school garden was half cinders, and grew very little other than the willow herb and chick-weed that readily takes over the sites of ruined buildings and industrial tips. The garden was crossed by the fumes from a nearby factory that processed oil. The fumes varied, of course, according to the breezes that blew. The fumes were always there; but sometimes they were so bad that I retreated with my class into the cleaner air of the classroom. Like most young teachers, I approached my work as if it were a crusade; though I was a little afraid of the antagonism of these strangers confined with me, yet I was convinced of something I had to give them. What I wanted to give was not more-or-less irrelevant information on how to grow this or that on soil in which it wouldn't grow, anyway; I wanted to give a sense of what the natural world meant to me. But I was not courageous enough to talk about such things when I was expected to give instructions on how to grow potatoes or, at best, to give elementary lessons in biology.

The significant part of my life was lived in the early morning, in the evening, and at weekend, in my cottage at Intake Farm; and in the quarter-acre garden that I cultivated there.

Intake Farm seemed, to the casual visitor, to be the most neglected of farms. And to the professional visitors—the cattle-feed salesman; the Milk Marketing Board official; the agent for the estate that owned the place; the butcher travelling to buy cheap meat—it appeared the same way. This small farm—sixty acres—was the most noticeable one from the other side of the valley because its fields were brilliant splashes of yellow dandelions, or white splashes of daisies; for Tommy never used selective weed-killers, nor did he ever plough his meadows for re-seeding. It seemed, within its close-hugging nest of sheds, litter of carts, middens, and piles of timber that he was always importing from demolition sites (he was saving them for fencing spars, though he was notorious for his ill-kept fences), to be like some backwash of jetsam cast into this hollow of the flowing fields. The paving stones of the lane had sunk at jagged angles, so that it was difficult to sweep them clean after a herd of cattle that tramped over them twice a day; and neither Tommy nor his wife Maggie found much time to clean the lane, anyway. One huge flat stone, that lay before his door (there was only one door to the house), was bright yellow from the regular scrubbing that Maggie gave it; but you could not reach that stone without wearing welling-ton boots to wade through the mud and cow-flops. Tommy, his working clothes faded to an overall khaki colour and stiffened with dried dung, was himself like a large cow-flop. His hedges were neglected for years. It did not occur to him to think that the time spent laying and cutting a hedge would be easily saved by not having to spend frequent, inconvenient days looking for strayed cattle. Intake Farm was the one place where blackberry bushes thickened the hedges so that they flowed loosely down the banks into the fields, with large gaps between that were closed with a loose strand of wire after the cattle had strayed—if Tommy remembered to close them at all.

These gaps, and the apparent air of neglect, encouraged trespassers. He guarded the main lane to the farm—a cindered track that ran through unfenced fields—by keeping there a bullock, who was

K

too young to be dangerous, but old enough to be intimidating, and who was, in fact, as friendly as a spaniel; he would go up to people on the lane in the hope that they would scratch his belly or his ears.

But Tommy's fields were crossed by several footpaths, which were the old routes to mills on the outskirts of hamlets, or buried somewhere in a wood, the houses that were once around them having scattered their stones over the ground.

If someone strayed from one of those confusing paths, and across Tommy's grassland, and he knew of it because the dog barked or because Maggie (who never rested during the day) told him of it, it was one of the few things that would disturb his afternoon sleep. (Every day, after midday dinner, he would sleep in front of the kitchen stove; during the winter, when winds blew around the house, he warmed his feet by stretching them into the oven.) He was most aggressive against trespassers in the spring, when the grass was growing. Whistling his dog and grasping his stick, he would go towards the trespassers, and stopping close enough to be heard but not so close that they might see how small he was, he would shout:

"Get off there! That's our living you's trampling on. 'Ave you no respect for folkses livelihood?"

If they were young, the trespassers ran off; if they were older they loped away, slowly, sullenly.

He was irrationally dedicated to the things that he loved. On the farm, there was no electricity; and no gas; and the water came from a spring. His interest in mechanical inventions had stopped in about 1935; there was an eccentric pump to bring water from the spring to the shippen (cowhouse); a hay-cutting machine, that looked like a grasshopper; and a petrol-driven motor to drive milking machines that rarely worked, and which he didn't wish to use, anyway. He loved horses, and kept two of them, expensively and well, though (except at haytime) he had work for only one of them. The reason that he did not have electricity—which the owner of the farm would have installed for him for only a slight rise in the rent—was not through meanness, but because he loved to milk his cattle primitively; and because he loved the ritual of lighting oil lamps.

To light a Tilley oil lamp, firstly he had to heat the gauze of the mantle by burning methylated spirit, soaked into padding held in a metal clip to the stem of the lamp. This lasted a few minutes whilst the blue flame died down and the gauze whitened with heat. Then he pumped to build up the pressure of the paraffin fume, slowly, slowly—if he pumped too hard the mantle burst into flames, thus destroying it—so that gradually more and more light was given out. This light awoke in a dark room like a flower opening in the morning.

Tommy got pleasure from this slow ritual; and that pleasure would have been lost had he been out of pace with the timing that it required.

And though he neglected so much, to the things that he cared about he gave this attention, this careful, joyous engrossment in their necessary pace.

He kept pigs because he could make money more easily from them than from any other stock; but he disliked pigs, so they were left uncleaned for weeks on end in the collapsing sheds and old railway waggons that drifted around his farm, whilst his two horses were stabled in solid stone stables that were as clean as hospitals, and decorated with fading prize-tickets from agricultural shows.

His way of disregarding jobs that ought to be done, but were not urgent, for the sake of giving his attention to whatever captivated him at the moment, was childish, and therefore exasperating— particularly to Maggie, for whom he was always calling to come and support him (rather than help him) at the variety of jobs that filled his day.

So, with the squawking of hens and grunting of pigs and the groan of cattle about the farm, "Maggie! Maggie! Maggie!" was a regular farmyard noise, as he "needed" her to hold a post that he was driving into the ground; to run back and forth with screws and hammer and spanner when he "mended" the patent drinking bowls for the cattle in the shippen; to bar the pigs from running in an unwanted direction when he was turning them from one pen to another.

This attractive childishness, somehow suited to his small size,

was perhaps the reason why neighbouring farmers indulged him
when he was a nuisance to them—as he often was, with his cattle
straying across their land, and his fields and hedgerows and the
courses of his brooks perpetuating clouds of weed seeds that drifted
across their pastures—or why they didn't despise him for his bad
farming practice. Amiably, they called him "Rancher"; but sometimes at an auction a farmer would get his own back, in a small way,
by selling to Tommy a cow too bony to sell to anyone else.

"I've just the beast for you, Tommy lad," someone would say
to him, "Just your price".

Tommy could tell a good cow from a bad one better than most
people could tell it. But he couldn't resist cheapness; nor the challenge
of proving that he could care for a sickly beast and turn it into a
plump one—which he often did; though sometimes his bargains
died, or were hastily sold for meat for zoo animals.

The different times of the year compelled him to work with their
seasonal urgencies. In dry summer weather, it was taking drums
of water to cattle in pastures that did not have a stream or a pond;
in winter it was shovelling snow so that he could take milk to the
end of the lane. Throughout any day of the year, his tendency for
childish dispersal of his energies was anchored by one or two un-
avoidable demands.

Maggie rose before him (though they both got up a little later
than most farmers do). He had to have the milk at the lane-end by
nine-thirty; so that compelled him to gulp a large mug of tea, and
go out to the shippen. Delivering his milk was the only thing that
made him take notice of time, and that compelled him to keep a
clock—a scratched and unpolished heirloom of a grandfather clock
ticking always twenty minutes fast in a dark corner of the hallway,
like a sinister visitor; and the clock was the only thing that made him
listen to the radio—so that he could set the clock twenty minutes
fast, by the radio's time signals.

Calling out to Maggie to do one job after another whilst he moved
with precise, instinctive timing, from the udders of one cow to those
of the next, he had the churns filled by nine o'clock, most days.

He spent twenty minutes harnessing one of the horses and loading the cart and crossing his fields to the public highway. (Nothing upset him as much as an unsympathetic lorry driver from the dairy, who would not delay a few minutes for him.)

When horse and man returned, both of them rested—the horse in the best pasture, or in the stable, according to the weather; and Tommy, after a heavy breakfast, sleeping on a chair with his feet on the stove.

Maggie was a restless, energetic woman who could not sleep during the day. At this time she cleaned the empty churns in the dairy, which was a bitterly unpleasant job without an efficient water supply; and very painful in winter.

In the late morning, Tommy made sporadic attempts at repairs around the farm, whilst Maggie fed the hens (Tommy sturdily thought of tending hens as women's work) and cooked a soporific midday meal, as well as she could with Tommy calling for her every few minutes.

After dinner, Tommy had another short sleep; sometimes Maggie rested then, by knitting, or by doing something in the house.

In the afternoon, Tommy harnessed the horse for a chore that depended on which day of the week it was. On Monday, he travelled the back doors of school kitchens, factory canteens, restaurants and greengrocers' shops, to collect swill for his pigs.

When he went out, one realized how incongruous he was in the modern world. At the farm he seemed as timeless as plants and animals; a peasant farmer could never have looked much different to him, and even his clothes looked like those I have seen in Breughel paintings. But, when riding his cart in the street, amongst cars and relatively smart people, he seemed utterly incongruous.

On Wednesday he did his "night soil" round. Many outlying farms and cottages did not have flush toilets; Tommy was paid a fee by the Cleansing Department to empty the buckets. It was called "night soil" because traditionally the lavatories were inoffensively emptied during the night. But Tommy did it during the afternoon.

It was said of him that he once dropped his jacket into a bin of night soil. He rolled up his shirt sleeve and plunged his arm into the bin. "Jacket's no good now," he said, "but I've got me sandwiches in the pocket."

On another afternoon he did errands for his trade in scrap metal; or he hauled another load of timbers from a demolished mill.

At the end of the afternoon, he hurriedly fed the pigs. It was usually late evening before he milked his cows again; at any rate, it was rare for him not to do it by the light of a paraffin lamp.

And once a month, he put on a neat black suit, after he'd finished the evening's milking, and he went ballroom dancing. He wore wellington boots through the mud to the end of the lane, and there he changed into dancing pumps, leaving his wellingtons under the stand for milk churns until he returned in the early hours of the morning.

It was only during hay-making time that this routine was much varied.

Then, a kind of fury overtook him.

He was always the first farmer in the district to attempt hay-making—not because he didn't know as well as anyone else that an early spell of sunshine might suddenly give way to rain, and ruin the cut grass; nor because he didn't realize that it was more economic to wait until the grass grew longer; it was simply that he couldn't resist the joy of hay-making. But he was usually a little later in starting than he intended, because his hay machine, which a wise man would have made sure was in working order well before hay-time, usually needed mending on that first sunny day that he thought about it, after it had been lying in the corner of a field all winter. He was sixty years old when I knew him; he had been working on farms since he could walk; but he had never learnt to prepare for hay-making.

Once he began hay-making, though, he was relentless. As his barn filled, it was as if he was seeing a magical fulfilment of his life and work. Milking the cattle was left until it was too dark to work in the hayfield; and as milking often took about two hours, it was often about two o'clock in the morning when he finished. Then he would feed the hens and the pigs, Maggie trotting behind him with the paraffin lamp.

Often and often, at around 3 a.m., instead of taking a little sleep, he would, if there was a moon or bright starlight to enable him to do it, go into a new field that had to be cut, and take advantage of the dew on the grass at that hour to scythe a way for his hay machine round the edge of the field—for you cannot use a scythe on dry grass.

Tommy neither smoked nor drank; this hay-making and the care of his horses were his drug and his intoxication.

Tommy was a tenant on the land his family had farmed for generations. One day, he leant on his ash stick in the yard, looking a little lost, as he often did during his working day, when he was wondering what job to do next. Tears drifted from his red eyes, caused, he said, by the March wind. He told me that the owners of Intake Farm had sold it for building land.

He carried on his work as usual, though a little lamely, for a while; but gradually both he and Maggie retreated more and more amongst their dark furnishings, until at last they were moved out to a council house on their own fields.

But until he left, he came out for just an hour or two each day, to repair door latches, fences, bits of walls, of property that was to be destroyed and that did not belong to him; that winter, because it was his habit to do so, he even manured his fields although they were to be built upon the following year.

Cattle waggons used to come into his yard about once a month, or even more rarely—he was always disturbed when his stock went to market, even though that was his living; also he hated the drivers coming because they carelessly grazed walls, knocked gate stumps, grazed the bark of trees. Now the lorries came every few days to rid him of his stock, including his bullock, until his yard and buildings were barren and empty and all that he could now do by way of mothering his loved farm was to scrub out the buildings, and scrub the stones of his yard (in a way he had never found time to scrub them before), though now there was only dust instead of the regular droppings of cattle.

The hens were sold as "chickens" to the Pakistanis who had a restaurant in town, and who regularly travelled the farms to buy poultry.

A site office was erected in the paddock. Because the farm gate was too narrow for them, bulldozers ripped through a wall and through half a dozen trees, churning the raw rough gap into mud so that they could park their site-clearing machinery in the yard.

Last of all, a vet took his dog behind the empty shippen and injected it. I went too, because the dog knew me and would follow me. Tommy stayed indoors, doubtless listening for a howl, for the last noise. There was silence.

I have not cultivated any land since I left Intake Farm; I had never done it before. The five years I spent there was the only period when I have experienced that delicious, close association with the earth, the weather, the seasons, the plants and other creatures, which comes from working with them to produce a minimal livelihood. So in ending my walk here, I had found my way back to a certain kind of root; to the closest contact I have ever had with the things I most care about. My memories are of physical work that seemed idyllic, because I was not employed by anyone, and because it was part of my happy emotions about the world that was around me. My memories are of the joy of laying a thorn hedge or of rhythmically driving a post into the ground; they are of learning to milk a cow, and of learning that a tender sensitivity must exist between the milker and the cow, if milk is to be drawn; of learning that there is a seasonal timing, that cannot be slowed or hurried, to the growth of plants; and they are of summer mornings, before I went to teach at Flowery Field. Then I would go out to my garden as it came light, maybe at half past five or at six o'clock, and hoe plants or mend a fence or collect eggs and clean out my hens, whilst I watched the

stars extinguish, and the grey, crepuscular light brighten, turn
slowly fiery, and suddenly be overcome by the great throbbing ball
of the sun. A little later I would hear our baby cry in the cottage,
or I would know that my wife had risen, when she lit the lamp in
the cottage, and the light of the lamp throbbed like a heart, like the
heart of the cottage, and then brightened, as if it shouted in the room;
I would see the light move into a lower room, as she came down-
stairs; and the sun would come so hot, even at six or seven o'clock
in the morning, that I would take off my shirt, and my shoes and
socks, and work. The rhythm of the work sent a glowing happiness
through my limbs. And through working regularly in a physical
way I learnt to be more tender in my handling of things. It is quite
impossible to work with a spade or a hoe or an axe or a spanner or a
scythe for more than an hour or two without getting crippling pains,
unless you discover and enter into a natural rhythm, dictated by the
tool you are handling, the things you are working with. Having discovered these rhythms of work, having discovered this exquisite,
gentle association with the world, it seemed that to be impatient;
to tear its symphonies of quiet sounds and movements, of birds and
animals and stirring plants and quiet tools, with impatient gestures;
to poison the land and its creatures with weed-killers and insect-
poisons; or excessively and brutally to formalize the land; or to
treat my own person crudely, to drink or to eat excessively, or to
smoke, was to profane some marvellous source of joy. It seemed that
every natural thing that I saw, smelled, or touched was numinous;
and it almost seemed that I would lose the sense of this if I did anything more excessive than drink water and eat simple food.

And, I am convinced, it was something like these feelings that
directed Tommy Toat, despite his fecklessness, his wayward scruffi-
ness, to cling to his way of life.

The extinction of Tommy Toat—and, with it, the extinction of my
own way of life, which I have found it so difficult to return to since—
was not an anomaly. It was part of the reckless destruction of an
unassessed and disregarded culture, which is being as relentlessly
destroyed here as anywhere else.

There is a much-used phrase that describes the loss of hold upon the land. "The moor's coming closer down every year," the old people, who are most often the people to notice it, say when they see what were patches of green cultivated field on the sides of the moor turning brown through neglect.

But here and there, long after the farmer has left and his house has been taken over by someone not interested in the land, you see patches of brighter green higher up the moor than they are seen in other places, so that they stand out; pastures that were so well cared-for, the moor finds it difficult to encroach upon them with its brown rushes and sour, dead grey grass.

Intake Farm shows in that way. And on its slightly brighter grass, a certain consciousness was born in me.

INDEX

INDEX